Destined

Destined

A Story *of* Resilience
and Beating *the* Odds

Aminata Sy

AMINATA SY ENTERPRISES, LLC

COPYRIGHT © 2025 AMINATA SY
All rights reserved. The views expressed herein belong solely to the author and do not necessarily reflect those of the U.S. government.

DESTINED
A Story of Resilience and Beating the Odds

FIRST EDITION

ISBN   978-1-5445-4718-3   *Hardcover*
          978-1-5445-4717-6   *Paperback*
          978-1-5445-4719-0   *Ebook*

*For my husband and children, who
have always been there for me.*

*For the other people who
have helped shape my life.*

*For all people everywhere who
dare to dream of a brighter day.*

Contents

PREFACE 9
1. MY ROOTS 11
2. A NEW COUNTRY, A NEW LIFE 25
3. THE TURNING POINT 47
4. JUGGLING IDENTITIES 77
5. EXPLORING MY GIFTS 109
6. SHAPING YOUNG MINDS 123
7. LEARNING ON THE JOB 139
8. RESILIENCE IN ADVERSITY 157
9. LANDING A DREAM CAREER 173
10. OUR COUNTRY AND ITS CONTRADICTIONS 195
11. HOW TO ACHIEVE AGAINST ALL ODDS 203
    ACKNOWLEDGMENTS 209
    ABOUT THE AUTHOR 213

Preface

September 2021

WHEN I IMMIGRATED TO THE UNITED STATES OF AMERICA in 2001, I was a high school dropout who didn't speak English and whose family, despite the very hard work of my husband and myself, was living below the poverty line. Today, I have a master's degree in public policy and work as a diplomat in the U.S. Department of State, helping to represent America to other nations of the world. This memoir is the story of that transformation.

My long-term professional goals were ambitions born out of both hope and fear for my family's future. I believed then, as I do now, that the United States of America is a country that offers people opportunities to make something out of their lives and to aspire to a better future for themselves and their families. However, my family and I were among the millions of people in America whose lives are defined by the day-to-day hardships of poverty and its limitations. The neighborhood we lived in, the places we went or couldn't go to, the schools my children attended, the food we ate, the people we interacted with, and the jobs available to my husband and me were all dictated by our financial status. So every day, I straddled hope and fear, believing that one day my family and I could have more control over our destinies but also that at any point something could happen that would stand in the way of those aspirations.

This book is for people who walk in the dark, not knowing if there will ever be light. This book is for women who constantly have to juggle the demands of their family, academic, and professional lives. This book is for the dreamers who have the audacity to believe that they can change their lives, the lives of their families, and beyond. This book is for every young person who has experienced poverty and disorienting change. I hope that my story will inspire you to transform your life, to walk in the dark and yet expect the light, to believe that you're the only one who can accomplish your life's mission, to have the courage to do it even though you're afraid, and to become a blessing for people near and far. The limitations in our lives are real, but the possibilities in our lives are also real. The question becomes, are we willing to turn our limitations into possibilities and take advantage of those possibilities to transform our lives?

Chapter One

My Roots

AT TEN YEARS OLD, I BECAME AN ADULT.

I was born bicultural and grew up multicultural. My mom left her home, Rwanda, in East Africa, and my dad his country, Senegal, in West Africa, in search of a better livelihood in Kinshasa, Zaire (renamed the Democratic Republic of Congo in 1997). This is where my parents met and married, and where I was born. I spent the first ten years of my life in Kinshasa, navigating the cultural differences encountered at school, with Congolese friends, and within my family. When speaking, my tongue moved between Lingala and French, and my ears became familiar with Pulaar, through my dad, and Kiswahili, through my mom.

When I was around the age of nine, my dad told me that he would send me to Senegal to a relative who was, he said, my aunt and namesake, because that was his native country and where I belonged. My dad had also told me that I wouldn't spend that much time in Senegal before returning for a visit, and I believed him. In September of 1990, at the age of ten, I separated from my parents at Kinshasa International Airport. Our group of family and friends gathered at a waiting area in the airport, all of us expecting Hadja, the wife of my dad's friend, who would be traveling with me to Dakar as my chaperone. I was wearing a pink dress with tiny white polka dots, pink ballerina shoes, and two flowery bow-shaped barrettes clipping my neatly braided hair.

My mom stood holding the hand of my younger brother, Abdoulaye, who was four years old. My dad zigzagged through the airport handling my documents and luggage, as I went around with our neighbor Rosa, joyfully exploring different locations. That was my first time at an airport and my first time seeing airplanes up close. Up to that point, I had only seen airplanes fly in the sky like birds and go so far up that they disappeared into the clouds. I couldn't wait to get on an airplane and experience what it felt like to be way up in the sky. By the time Hadja arrived, I was ready to go, and passengers had started boarding the plane. Abdoulaye was clueless about what was happening; he asked my mom if I was leaving and if he could go with me. My mom couldn't contain her sorrow and cried the entire time at the airport as my dad and others consoled her. But I didn't understand my situation well enough to be sad; instead, I was giddy with anticipation. My body stood at the airport, but my mind had already gone into the airplane. I didn't realize it, but that was my last day in Kinshasa, my last day of being a child.

Only days after I landed at Dakar's Léopold Sédar Senghor International Airport in Senegal, my beaming face had been replaced with a dull expression, and the adrenaline rush of boarding an airplane transformed into the realization that I had begun a new, strange journey. When I first met my aunt—Yaye, as her children and grandchildren called her and I later did as well (it means "mother" in Wolof and Pulaar)—it was very clear to me as a ten-year-old that she didn't have the economic means or the physical capacity to take care of me, that she was a grandmother who depended on others to survive. Speaking in Pulaar as someone translated into French, Yaye told me that she had nothing but her family members and visited them frequently, that she wanted a child who listened, followed her guidance, and remained where she told her. These were among her first words to me. I felt that I needed to listen to Yaye because she was already living in a tough situation, and I didn't want to worsen it for her.

Yaye lived in the neighborhood named Medina, in a two-story house owned by a relative of hers who lived there with her family and tenants, all residing under the same roof. The downstairs had seven rooms, including Yaye's room, and a photography studio. Most of the downstairs rooms were occupied by tenants—some couples, others single. The roofless upstairs opened wide to the clear skies with a comprehensive view of the neighborhood. At the center of the upstairs area, there was a spacious terrace, where people ate lunch and dinner, washed clothes, or simply spent time socializing. On one side of the terrace was a bathroom and toilet and on its other side a cage with pigeons flying in and out and flocking through the area while munching on millet grains on the concrete floor.

The owner of the house, a grandmother with many children and grandchildren, resided in the living quarters on one side of the terrace near a kitchen and a row of four rooms. Only family members or visiting relatives of the homeowner lived upstairs, no tenants. Yaye's cramped bedroom fit a queen-size bed, a brown freestanding closet about eighty inches tall and twenty inches wide, and an incense burner near the door.

The Medina neighborhood was densely populated and always bustling. Near the entrance of the house where Yaye resided, there was a mosque from which the call to prayer was issued five times a day. The road right outside the house was packed with cars, buses, and taxis riding up and down at all hours. Across the street, people formed long lines to fetch water at a public faucet. Some businesses in the neighborhood sold ready-made outfits while others sewed tailor-made clothes. At the nearby market, vendors sold butchered lamb and beef, vegetables, fruits, and freshly prepared peanuts in hot sand, served on pieces of newspaper.

Most days, I sat for hours curled up in a corner of my aunt's room, my knees pulled up to my chest. To calm my sorrow, I sang in Lingala the songs of singer Papa Wemba. Like a raging rain, tears rolled down my face nonstop. "May God protect me from your tears," Yaye would say to me. "Do you want to go back to your parents? Did you think that you were coming to a lavish lifestyle? I am destitute. I have nothing but my family members." I wondered what I was doing in Senegal. I didn't know anyone in Senegal. I didn't know Yaye; she didn't know me. Yaye couldn't support herself and certainly couldn't support me. Why didn't Yaye tell my dad that she didn't have the means to support me? Why was I living like an orphan when my parents were alive and well?

Yaye and I couldn't communicate directly. She spoke Pulaar and Wolof; I spoke Lingala and French. Every morning, Yaye would ask a young male relative who lived in a room adjacent to hers to translate her Pulaar to me and my French to her. "Please help me with this child. She doesn't understand anything I'm saying," Yaye would tell the young man. Many of these exchanges took place until I began picking up Pulaar and Wolof.

Inside of me, I had become a grown-up. I no longer played with dolls; instead, I worried. I thought about how my behavior in Dakar could impact my mom and my dad in Kinshasa. If I misbehaved, my parents would hear about it, and that would upset them. I needed to be patient and tolerate the situation. After all, my dad had spent a lot of money and energy to get me there. I didn't know much about my aunt's past, as it was not part of the family discussion, only that her sons, who were living overseas, often sent her money to support her. Her daughter rented a room across from the house Yaye lived in and had three sons and a daughter my age. Suddenly, in Dakar, I had a much larger family, filled with relatives I had never heard of.

At school, I was the foreign kid who spoke French. Some students made fun of me for not speaking Wolof and for being a foreigner, especially in what was supposed to be my own country; others thought that I was interesting because I spoke French. I could barely interact with my peers because all of them spoke Wolof, though they generally understood French. On the other hand, I carried out long conversations with my teachers. In Dakar, people usually spoke in Wolof and their ethnic languages. French was the official language imposed on the country by its former French colonizers and taught in schools but not necessarily spoken fluently by students, especially during the early years at school.

In Kinshasa, I lived with my parents and Abdoulaye on a vibrant street named Bagata. My parents rented a one-bedroom apartment with a living room on the opposite side of the living quarters of the homeowner, who resided in a three-bedroom unit with his family. I had my own bed, mosquito net, sheets, and covers. My mom cooked in a large outdoor space in front of the apartment, open to the blue skies on the mostly sunny days, and behind it stood trees of avocado, mango, and palm oil nuts. Outside of the house stretched Bagata Street, and across from it spread a garden where people cultivated different plants, such as that of cassava. Next door was a hotel; the owner and his family lived on the ground level, and the other floors were for guests. The Matongé night market nearby ran from evening to the next morning and was packed with people and vendors, many selling grilled meats and fish. My dad's store was located at Kanda Kanda Avenue, a short walking distance from the apartment, and also where popular Congolese singer Papa Wemba used to reside (he moved to France in the 1980s). The singer's rumba music seemed omnipresent.

By contrast, the soundtrack of my life in Dakar was provided by the haunting voice and wistful melodies of Senegalese singer Baaba Maal. Yaye woke up with her radio at 4:00 a.m. and went to bed with it at around 10:00 p.m. She listened to local, national, and international news, switching through different stations and only taking a break from her radio during her daily visits to the homes of relatives and friends. At breakfast time, around 8:00 a.m., she listened to local news on the same station that played the Baaba Maal song titled in Pulaar "Diahowo," or "Traveler."

Baaba Maal released "Diahowo" on his 1991 album *Baayo*, an album that spoke to the singer's longing for his homeland as he traveled the world to perform. The song "Diahowo" began with the sound of the calm sea, followed by crashing waves. As he sang, Baaba Maal seemed to speak to listeners in his harmonious back-and-forth with his background singer, Mansour Seck. I didn't understand what Baaba Maal was saying; however, the conversational tone of his lyrics calmed my internal anxieties. The song invoked feelings of nostalgia that I had no vocabulary for. All I knew was that I wanted and needed to hear "Diahowo." The whole song seemed to say, "This is an urgent message. Listen." And I did.

Through Baaba Maal's song, which felt so much like a group lament, I mourned my childhood in Kinshasa through the soundtrack of my life in Dakar. It made me think of my mom and life in Kinshasa. He kept me company while taking me to a familiar place. I remembered the afternoons I sneaked into my parents' room and played dress-up. The brown dresser, with its rectangular mirror, faced the queen-size bed. Beneath the mirror was a shelf, where my mom organized her jewelry and makeup. I applied her shimmering brown powder to my face and a touch of her clear lipstick to my lips. I put on her dangling gold earrings, necklace, and bangles. I walked back and forth in her room like a model strutting down the runway. I enjoyed the feeling of looking like a beautiful woman. Most days, my mom was busy with house chores, so she didn't notice the dress-up episodes. And when she noticed, she didn't mind.

I remembered the afternoons I held Abdoulaye's hand walking to my dad's store. My dad gave us cans of condensed Nestlé's milk when we were at the store. Abdoulaye and I would rush home to indulge in the milk. My mom would hand us two pieces of white bread. We would cut them open and drizzle the gooey, sweet milk on them. We would bite into our mouthwatering pieces of bread, dripping with milk, and would wish they could last longer.

I remembered the late nights my dad returned home with grilled lamb called dibi. The aroma of the meat filled the apartment, as my mom unwrapped the brown paper bag. We sat around our small living-room table watching TV as we ate the tender pieces of dibi. Abdoulaye and I never knew when it would be dibi night but always hoped for it. I remembered the moments I played with dolls and jumped rope with my friend Nicole.

In 1991, my dad came to Dakar. I thought once he saw that Yaye couldn't support me, he would take me back to Kinshasa with him. Instead, he pretended that my living situation with Yaye was normal. The fact that I didn't have a place of my own in that room was okay. The fact that Yaye couldn't provide food or clothes for me was okay. The fact that Yaye and I struggled to communicate was okay.

He brought a cassette tape with a message from my mom. He shared the message with me while I visited him at the home of the relative with whom he stayed while he was in Dakar. We sat on a mat on the house's veranda, surrounded by other people. My dad played my mom's message, which said in part, "I encourage you to be patient with your situation. Don't give up on your schooling. Do everything you can not to forget Lingala. I know no other language in which we can speak. Your departure is giving me a lot of pain. I am sending you warm greetings." Hearing my mom's voice triggered fresh nostalgia. My dad interrupted the cassette tape a few times to tell me to stop crying. But the sound of my mom whipping through her words made me cry harder because I missed her and missed living with her. I sensed in her voice the toll our separation took on her—the toll of not knowing when she would reunite with her child again.

A part of me continued to hope that my dad would feel sorry for his decision and return me to Kinshasa. But his visit to Senegal was the last time I saw him.

After I left Kinshasa, my parents lived through years of hardship. My mom sank into sadness from my absence but soon surrendered to her fate and moved on with life. She told me years later that girls and women in Kinshasa, including girls from the immigrant Senegalese community, were constant victims of rape, which remained a source of worry for parents, but she and my dad couldn't explain that situation because I was too young. My mom said the main reason my dad sent me to Senegal was to protect me from such violence, and that was why she agreed to the decision. My dad never intended to keep me away from them for years, she said. She insisted that life circumstances dictated our extended separation and that "a person cannot escape from destiny." I took in my mom's explanation but believed that it was parents' responsibility to take care of their children, which would not include handing over that responsibility to someone else to execute on their behalf. Over the next decade in Kinshasa, my parents lived through civil wars, unrest, rioting, looting, lack of money, and unemployment. My parents and I rarely communicated over those years because of their unstable circumstances.

Gloomy is how I describe my teenage years. Separating from my parents at the age of ten and moving from Kinshasa to Dakar meant that I had to grow up overnight. I became isolated in every way: figuring out life in a context unknown to me, learning to adapt daily, trying to survive through the limitations of poverty, living in dual worlds in my mind but having no control either of the past or present, and certainly not the future. I was confused, lonely, and in pain.

Remaining in school was an ongoing struggle. I repeated fourth grade and attended the sixth grade three times before finally earning the mandatory diploma for that level. I passed ninth grade on the second try. Yaye, her daughter, her grandchildren, and I moved into a house together in the neighborhood of Sicap Liberté 4. I attended Blaise Diagne high school, which required transportation, lunch, clothes and shoes, and school supplies, all of which Yaye could barely provide. Every morning, Yaye bickered about giving me the equivalent of twenty cents for transportation to and from school and told me to eat lunch at the home of one or another family member who resided near the high school. On any given week, I would have lunch at four or five different houses, return to school during the afternoons for classes, and then go home. I also ate lunch often at the house of my friend Assy, who lived with her grandmother and siblings and welcomed me with open arms. Assy and I shared many grades, grew close, and spent most of our time together in between classes and during recess. She was an easygoing friend who focused on her education and her family. Like Assy, my life also revolved around school and home.

By the time I was in tenth grade, I could no longer learn and had enough of school and its routine. All of my traumas seemed to come together and block my mind. I went to classes but heard nothing and understood nothing of what the teachers taught. I didn't lack intelligence or a desire to learn; I lacked the means and conditions for study and was drowning ever deeper in my sorrows. In tenth grade, I dropped out of school, believing that was the end of my education.

Yaye wanted to raise me in a decent way but struggled through many limitations. She had a big heart and was proud that my dad named me after her and sent me to Dakar to be raised by her. However, she was confronted with the daily harsh realities of poverty and dependence on others and dealt with responsibilities connected to her daughter and grandchildren, who also needed her support. Yaye's situation didn't allow her to properly fulfill her desire to raise me in good conditions, though she tried. She enrolled me in school after school as I repeated grades, so I could continue my education. She asked her neighborhood friends to braid me, so my hair was taken care of. She connected me with a peer who lived nearby and spoke fluent French, so I could befriend her and have someone to interact with. She asked her relatives for used clothes and shoes for me, so I could have something to wear. She fed me through the support of her relatives, so I could have nutrition for my body. Yaye, with the support of her daughter, tried to raise me well and did her best under her circumstances, and for that, I'll always be grateful to her and her daughter.

Yaye expressed regard for me and words of blessings when we lived together, but especially after we separated. I spoke with Yaye over the phone at least once or twice a month when I immigrated to America, and during our conversations, she would repeat similar words to me. "You listened to me; you stayed where I told you and went where I told you," she would say. "You could have become a child who did whatever you wanted, but you didn't. May God shield you, the way you shielded me. May God bless you." Yaye meant that she could barely care for me, yet I still followed her guidance, which shielded her from being criticized by others, especially relatives, about how she was raising me. When I became a mother, Yaye added to her prayers. "May God bless you and your family and every child you give birth to."

I wanted to find an honorable way to get off of Yaye's hands, both for her sake and my parents', and the only way I could think of was marriage. I could have gotten caught up in drugs and alcohol, prostitution, or teen pregnancy; somehow, I avoided all of those traps. At the age of nineteen, I married Abdoul, whom I had met the year prior when he came from America, where he lived and worked, to vacation in Dakar. He had struck me as a responsible man. He had never courted me, and we had never dated. In Senegal, such a marriage was nothing unusual; many people married young and without having dated.

I continued to live with Yaye while I applied for a U.S. visa, which I later received. My husband, Abdoul, came to pick me up in Dakar during the summer of 2001. From the time I went to Yaye in 1990 to the time I left her in 2001, I rarely heard from my parents. Hadja, who had chaperoned me to Senegal when I was ten, took on the role of godmother in my life, a relationship that Yaye encouraged. She kept an eye on me over the years and supported me financially, such as in buying my back-to-school clothes and shoes. I spent some summer breaks at Hadja's home, an environment of luxury and abundance, which exposed me to a different way of living. She was a businesswoman, who owned a high couture boutique in downtown Dakar, sewing Senegalese clothes for an elite clientele. Hadja's consistent advice to me was to stay in school and study because education was very important. I believed her, but I was a wounded teenager who felt that I couldn't continue with my schooling.

That summer, Hadja paid for and organized my wedding ceremony, which took place at her home and went very well. My clothes were specifically sewn for the occasion. For the wedding reception, I wore a beautiful Senegalese-style long white dress with crystal-like studs throughout the soft material. On the neck section of the dress were eight circular light-peach pearls. I accompanied the dress with closed-toe and open-back white high-heeled shoes, a small white clutch handbag, and dazzling silver jewelry: earrings, a necklace, and two bangles on my right arm. My hair was styled in a chignon, surrounded by tiny white barrettes with pearls; the hair pulled together toward the top of my head, and some hair dangled on one side of my face. My makeup and nails had been done for the occasion. A crowd of family and friends attended, plentiful and delicious foods were served, and entertainment was provided throughout the day. The reception was hosted on the rooftop of a house across from Hadja's, and gifts were received in abundance.

I took a monumental step without knowing what to expect from my marriage or from living in America, but I knew that I needed a change in my life and went for it anyway.

Growing up without my parents remains one of the most painful experiences of my life; it's also one of the experiences from which I learned the most. In our lives, we all face adversities and have to decide how to respond to them. I decided to honor my parents and my aunt because the people who are supposed to take care of us and protect us may not completely fulfill their responsibilities, but they still deserve our gratitude and consideration. I decided to adapt to my circumstances because that was the only way I knew to survive. I later decided to forgive anyone who hurt me during my childhood and started my healing process.

As human beings, we have a quiet strength that can carry us through pain and suffering. I just happened to tap into that strength early in my life. I learned that difficult situations can't break me, that I'm stronger than anything life throws at me, and that the strength in me is in each of us.

Chapter Two

A New Country, a New Life

IN JULY 2001, AT TWENTY-ONE YEARS OLD, I DEPARTED Dakar with my husband and flew to John F. Kennedy International Airport in New York City to begin a new life in America. We settled in a one-bedroom apartment on the west side of Philadelphia, Pennsylvania, where my husband had already lived for years and worked as a manager at a parking garage company. He had no family members in Philadelphia, only some friends and acquaintances from the Senegalese and Mauritanian immigrant communities in our neighborhood. My husband and I didn't know one another; I was a naive young woman, and he was a seasoned man, but we had a similar vision for our lives. We both wanted to build a life together that included children, a stable home, and a source of income, along with commitment to and support of one another. "If I can get the moon for you, I will," my husband told me. He has maintained that good intention to this day and is a significant blessing in my life and an outstanding father. My husband has been consistently supportive of me throughout my experiences in America but prefers remaining behind the scenes; that's why I don't speak of him as much as I would really like to in this book. I started life in Philadelphia clueless about what the future held but hopeful that tomorrow would be better than yesterday.

I was eight and a half months pregnant and running a restaurant when everything changed.

Our restaurant, Le Dakar, was located on Baltimore Avenue in West Philadelphia, along with other shops and restaurants and many African businesses. A few months after I joined my husband in Philadelphia, we opened the restaurant, wanting to make a living as a couple by serving the many people in the African immigrant community, especially men who sold their merchandise, including handbags, belts, and watches on the nearby streets and women who worked as hair braiders in the neighborhood salons. My husband stopped working at his job as a parking garage manager to embark on this new undertaking.

Our apartment was above the restaurant. His days started at 4:00 a.m. when he went to an Italian market in South Philadelphia to buy fish and vegetables for our various dishes; mine started at 6:00 a.m. when I began to cook and prepare the restaurant for service. Both of our workdays ended at midnight after we closed and cleaned up the restaurant. My movements revolved around the apartment, the restaurant, and the three shops next to Le Dakar. I mainly interacted with customers from Senegal, Mauritania, Ivory Coast, Mali, and Guinea, and only later did I begin to encounter native-born Americans as well. I spoke Pulaar, Wolof, and French and was starting to learn some English.

One Sunday afternoon in September 2002, while my husband ran the restaurant, I attended a childbirth ceremony held by a member of the Senegalese community whose wife had given birth to a daughter and who invited us to the event. My husband had known this man for years and wanted at least one of us to celebrate the arrival of his first child. Almost near the term of my pregnancy, I felt like a pumped balloon, my breath short and heavy, my face covered with pimples, my dark brown skin turned charcoal black, my feet swollen to twice their normal size and no longer fitting into sandals, my blood pressure staying at 180 or higher, and my weight about 195 pounds. Since the fourth month of my pregnancy, I had no longer slept at night. Instead, I watched Senegalese comedy sketches to keep me company; sometimes my husband watched with me; sometimes he slept. Most nights, the baby's movements were visible on the surface of my skin. I held my stomach as I twisted and turned.

The ambiance of the ceremony seemed to bring together all the discomforts of my aching back and feet, suffocated breath, banging headaches, and puffy body. The loud music penetrated my head; the crowd of people conversing worsened my pounding headache. I escaped to a bedroom away from the noises to isolate myself. A few women came to check on me, and I told them that I needed a ride home and that I felt like I was losing my mind with the headaches, so my husband's friend drove me home. Once home, my husband drove me to the Hospital of the University of Pennsylvania. As soon as we arrived, a nurse took my blood pressure and said it was too high and that both the baby and I were in danger. Surrounded by wires and machines, I lay in the intensive care unit, where doctors induced my delivery process. The doctors said that if they waited for a normal delivery, the baby and I could die. So they plugged me into a ventilator, an IV machine, and monitors for my blood pressure, oxygen level, and heart, as well as for the condition of the baby, as they prepared the operating room for my cesarean section.

I lay on the bed, facing the ceiling, my right arm pricked with a syringe left in place for repeated blood draws. My tears poured like a heavy rain as I screamed, "My head hurts, it's too much; my head hurts, it's too much!" My husband sat near me, stuck between trying to console me and processing his terror. My severe high blood pressure triggered a seizure that left me unconscious. I no longer knew myself or my surroundings. After the doctors and nurses helped me through the seizure, my husband came to see me, and I asked him, "Who are you?" He left the room wondering, "What if I lost both my wife and baby at the same time?" I had come to the United States in July 2001; now, fourteen months later, in September 2002, my husband found himself pondering that worst-case scenario. Fortunately, I gradually regained my memory, as doctors and nurses tried different medications to lower my blood pressure.

Soon, I was in the operating room; the doctors administered an epidural and then performed a cesarean. My husband stood near my head, witnessing everything; I barely felt anything. We soon welcomed baby Amadou to the world! The tiny baby screamed, eager for warmth. I mustered a smile, relieved that at last, my son had made it into the world, but still I worried about his health and mine. I wondered, "Will I make it out of this hospital to take care of my baby? Is my baby okay?" The nurses wrapped Amadou and helped me hold him, but I was so weak I could hardly do it. My husband held our baby with pride; now he was the father of a son. Amadou had jaundice, a medical condition that turned his skin and eyes yellow, so he stayed under a light for hours every day to treat it. I remained hooked up to an IV and to machines to give me supplementary oxygen while doctors tried different blood pressure medicines to treat my postoperative pain caused by the operation and high blood pressure. I was diagnosed with preeclampsia, a medical condition caused by chronic hypertension during pregnancy. The doctors said I couldn't breastfeed my baby because the many medications had poisoned my milk.

My husband went back and forth to the hospital, visiting me and baby Amadou while still managing the restaurant. I managed Le Dakar's day-to-day operations, from cooking and supervising other cooks to taking orders and payments, plating meals, and serving customers. My husband bought our dishes' ingredients, made deliveries to customers who had ordered from their businesses, and paid the staff and the bills.

After Amadou's birth, I stayed in the hospital for two weeks, during which time I experienced another seizure. When three men, my husband's acquaintances from the Senegalese community, came to visit me at the hospital, I didn't remember their visits, even though my husband said I talked to them. The combination of the different medicines in my body and the impact of the seizure kept me physically present but mentally absent. Not one woman in the Senegalese immigrant community in West Philadelphia visited me and my baby, not even the couple whose childbirth ceremony triggered my premature delivery. Why? I don't know. The only woman who visited me was Keisha, an immigrant from Poland who was a customer at Le Dakar. Keisha found me in deep sleep and left fresh flowers and a handwritten note wishing me well. When I read her note, I had a brief flashback to my days at Le Dakar, greeting customers in my novice English, "Welcome! How can I help you?" or in my confident French, "Comment ça va, mon frère, qu'est ce que vous voulez commander?" or in Pulaar, "No banda ada seli, ko djinoda hande?" or in Wolof, "Nanga def, lan ngay jende tay?" I switched back and forth between customers, languages, and cultures. I enjoyed interacting with people, cooking, and serving dishes. For a moment, I forgot the hospital environment and remembered some pleasurable times running Le Dakar. Keisha loved Senegalese culture; she had learned French while working in the Peace Corps in Senegal. She often came to eat at Le Dakar with her friends, and we had long conversations in French.

Memories of Le Dakar still lingered in my mind. One particular incident was especially vivid. One afternoon in early 2002, a White man came to the restaurant, different from all the customers whom I had served up to that point. I greeted him with warmth, as I did every customer, and shared our menu with him. Le Dakar offered twelve African dishes on the menu, and one dessert of sour cream mixed with millet grains named *thiakiri*. Its beverages included three homemade drinks: a tangy, sweet, red juice called *bissap*, made out of hibiscus; a ginger juice, spicy and sweet combined with a dash of pineapple and lemon; and a hot green tea with mint, prepared Senegalese style, called *ataya*.

I used to cook most of those dishes in Senegal and was eager to share them with the Philadelphia community. The man ordered a little bit of everything: the sauces all served with white rice, such as the caramelized onions with chicken (*Yassa*), the thick green stew of cassava leaves, and the rich, creamy peanut butter sauce, as well as the most prominent Senegalese dish, *thiebou djeun*, or fried rice with fish and vegetables. He didn't tell me who he was or what his intentions were. I took his orders and served him the dishes, and he tasted them one at a time.

By that point, I had served many customers, most of them from Mali, Ivory Coast, Guinea, Senegal, and Mauritania. Sometimes we had White customers, and their absolute favorite was our *dibi*, or charcoal-grilled lamb, and our *thiebou djeun*. Those White customers either ate in the restaurant or ordered something to take home. A couple of them started ordering only the *roff*, fresh parsley blended with cloves of garlic, salt, and black and red peppers, that we inserted inside the fish of the *thiebou djeun*. But no one before had ordered six or seven dishes, in small portions, at the same time or had asked so many questions about the meals and their ingredients.

When my husband returned to the restaurant from delivering meals, I told him about this White man and his many food orders. I added that it was a bit strange that he came to taste the food but not really to eat. He reassured me that it wasn't a big deal. This same White man came back another day, this time with a friend. They ordered at least six dishes, the *thiakiri* dessert, and the *bissap* drink. The two men tasted all the meals while they chatted.

The White man returned again a third time and ordered one dish and *thiakiri*. This time he told me he wanted to interview me and my husband about our work. When we met, my husband insisted on knowing who he was before answering his questions. He pulled out his business card and said he would make an exception from his usual practice of remaining anonymous in his work. He said he was Craig LaBan, a food critic with the *Philadelphia Inquirer,* and that he generally didn't reveal his identity to restaurant owners while he was evaluating their restaurant and cuisine. Craig asked more questions about the flavors in Le Dakar's meals, Senegalese culture, the music we played, and the *bissap* and ginger juices. He was a pleasant man, genuinely interested in our cooking and knowledgeable about flavors. Since I was still learning English, my husband translated much of his conversation for me, but I understood many of his questions and sometimes replied to them.

At the end of our interview, Craig told us that he would write about Le Dakar, and when his article about our restaurant was published, we would have a rush of customers that we needed to prepare for. I didn't know about the *Philadelphia Inquirer* or its influence, so I didn't take Craig's advice seriously. We also set a date that Craig would send a photographer to take photos of our dishes and of my husband and me.

On March 3, 2002, Craig's article, titled, "Le Dakar: Home Cooking, Direct from Senegal," was published in the *Philadelphia Inquirer,* and our phone started ringing nonstop. Callers would say things like, "I read about you and your restaurant in the *Inquirer*. I want to order *yassa*. You know, the dish with the caramelized onions?" From that point on, White customers came to eat at the restaurant in droves, especially for dinner.

We were soon overwhelmed. We had never had that many customers all at once; we didn't have the necessary support staff; the orders surpassed our capacity to prepare and serve them. Le Dakar had seating for twenty-eight people and took customers on a first-come, first-served basis. From around 7:00 p.m. to 10:00 p.m., customers packed Le Dakar, and others waited in line outside for open seats. We hired two more people, a server and a cook, to help with the sudden increase in customers.

Le Dakar was also featured in *Philadelphia* magazine's "Best of Philadelphia" issue in August 2002, where it was mentioned as the reviewers' favorite among the city's international restaurants.

I had the pleasure of cooking and serving delicious dishes daily and of meeting new people, trying to speak my bare-bones English, as they constantly told me, "You're doing good!" We were able to keep up with our bills and staff salaries until I was hospitalized, and that's when the business slowed down drastically. But we couldn't sustain the restaurant long-term without my husband and me at full capacity to work.

Even though I was fighting to regain strength after Amadou's birth, I still hoped that somehow we could keep the restaurant open. But I also knew our situation too well to kid myself. I knew that the end of Le Dakar was near and that there was no turning back. My husband and I were embarking on a new reality, parenthood, and we had to face that, even if we barely had the answers. I was supposed to walk through other doors, to live out other experiences, but I couldn't see that possibility at that point, only years later when I looked back. Life is always talking to us and showing us the path, if we're willing to hear, see, and believe in its process.

During my hospitalization, every day, every hour, seemed the same; the distinctions between days of the week as well as night and day were gone. On the clock facing my hospital bed, the hands moved, but I couldn't tell the difference between eight in the morning and eight at night. The lights were always on and always bright. Nurses and doctors walked in and out of the hospital rooms and performed blood pressure checks, temperature checks, blood draws, and more blood drawings. Nurses brought baby Amadou to me at least once a day to hold and bottle-feed him. The hospital routine, my unstable health and that of my baby, and my husband's efforts to hold on to Le Dakar for just one more day all flooded my mind. I wondered, "Will my son have a mother to care for him? How can we make it as a family and as new parents?"

I did everything in bed with the help of nurses. I couldn't shower or get out of bed because of the many machines hooked up to me and my weak body. One day, I told a nurse that I couldn't stand my own body anymore and asked if she could help me shower. She brought towels, water, and body wash and sat me up on the bed. She washed, rinsed, and dried my entire body. When the nurse was done, my mind and body felt lighter. A revived sense of life awoke in me that the sickness and hospital environment had taken away. I thanked the nurse for helping me feel better.

Then came the day when a doctor said he would help me get out of bed and walk. My heart pounded in fear—boom boom, boom boom; my body trembled. I wondered, "Can my legs stand anymore? Can I walk anymore?" I set one foot on the floor, then the other, as the doctor held my hand. My eyes began to see tiny, navy-blue spots; my head spun like a merry-go-round. I paused and sat on the bed. The doctor asked, "Can you stand? How are you feeling?" I twirled my pointing right finger to illustrate the dizziness. The doctor held my waist and placed my left hand around his shoulders to lift me off the bed. I stood! Then the doctor showed me how to place one foot in front of the other, so he could check my balance. My legs continued to shake, my head continued to spin, and my eyes continued to see navy-blue spots, but I managed about ten steps. For the first time in over a week, I stood, and I walked!

From then on, every day a doctor supported me as I stood and walked. About twelve days into my hospitalization, a group of doctors, at least ten, came together into the room while my husband was there. They each talked about the treatments I had received and the progress I had made, and they decided that I was ready to return home. My husband translated much of that information for me. I didn't know what to think or how to feel. On the one hand, I was relieved that I would soon be going home to continue living my life. On the other hand, I was still sick and had a newborn baby to take care of and no support, except for my husband. The two of us didn't know what we were doing and didn't have the money to care for our baby. Amadou had about two more days left of his treatment for jaundice, so I asked the doctors if I could stay at the hospital and be with my baby as much as possible.

The doctors transferred me to a guest suite at the hospital that looked more like a hotel room, with a bed, couch, and bathroom. From there, nurses took turns escorting me in a wheelchair to baby Amadou in the mornings and the afternoons. With the help of nurses, I held my son and bottle-fed him, staying with him for at least two hours during each visit.

I felt grateful that my baby and I had both survived our ordeal. Something in me had shifted; I felt a new sense of purpose. Now, I was responsible for another human being. I knew what it was like to live without my mother or father, and I absolutely didn't want that for my child. I wanted to be there for my son and do everything in my power to take care of him.

After my visits, the nurses returned my baby to his therapeutic lights. The extra days that Amadou and I stayed at the hospital gave my husband a little more time to sort out how he would welcome us home. About fourteen days into our hospital stay, doctors discharged me and my baby. My husband picked us up, strapped our son into his blue car seat, and drove us to our apartment on Baltimore Avenue. I believed that God was with me in those difficult moments, though previously I didn't always believe in his power and thought I was alone. God had shown me his power; my baby and I were alive and going home.

With less money coming into Le Dakar, my husband had to decide whether to close the restaurant, and if not, how to pay the bills and the salaries of three cooks, two servers, and a dishwasher. He had to figure out how our one-bedroom apartment would accommodate the three of us. We hadn't bought baby items yet, and even so, Le Dakar's revenue had already slipped away, with fewer dishes cooked and fewer customers buying. Without my support, it was only a matter of days before he closed the restaurant for good.

By the time my baby and I arrived home, my husband had closed the restaurant and let go of the employees. We had no source of income. I walked with my back slightly bent over from the lingering cesarean pain and the preeclampsia. My blood pressure levels had started to return to normal, but the dizziness continued, and all of my teeth wiggled. I became terrified that I would wake up one day and find my mouth empty of teeth. My baby and I came home to our cold one-bedroom apartment with no crib, no baby clothes, no diapers, no wipes, or anything else that showed the presence of a newborn. My husband and I dressed our baby in hospital clothes and diapers; we kept him warm with hospital blankets, and he drank hospital milk.

My husband went to get information about government assistance for food for babies and mothers. In the days that followed, we received milk for our son and cereal and milk for me. From then on, I lived mainly on Rice Krispies and milk. My teeth still wiggled, so I was relying on milk's calcium to strengthen them. I bottle-fed my baby with milk from the government's Women, Infants, and Children program. My husband fixed meals for us from the leftover frozen foods from Le Dakar.

We owed over $100,000 in hospital bills and started to receive thirty to forty collection calls per day demanding payment. Meanwhile, our baby cried day and night; calming him down became my number one goal. When we took Amadou to our local clinic for a checkup, the doctor told us that he looked fine and that he simply liked to cry.

I continued to take medications for blood pressure and pain relief, about seven different kinds, and to limp around the apartment from the aftereffects of the cesarean. My body remained weak while the hollerings of my baby, the ringing of the phone, and the uncertainties about our survival as a family caused my stress level to soar. I asked myself, "How will we make it out of this situation?" Soon, we moved to a four-story apartment building at 47th and Locust Streets in West Philadelphia, which was cheaper. My husband had salvaged what he judged important from the restaurant, from pots and pans to frozen foods, like the big chicken legs that featured in many of our dishes.

The collection calls for my hospital bills continued, and my son continued to holler. I bathed him, sang for him, talked to him, kept him warm, rocked him back and forth in my arms, and later carried him on my back to calm him down. But my baby kept crying most of the time. One night, I laid him in his car seat and talked to God, hoping something would change, and tears started to roll down my face as I prayed, "God, I've done everything I can for my baby to stop crying. I'm tired; I'm sick. I don't know what to do with my baby. No matter what I do, he keeps crying. God, help me." Motherhood is a humbling experience that reminds us just how much we don't control in our lives, even with our best efforts.

I was twenty-two years old, still limping around the apartment with pain. My husband was on a furious hunt for a job, any job that would pay him enough to keep us in that apartment and help us buy infant formula and diapers. He filed for bankruptcy to protect us from our debts, as we continued to struggle. The tenants of the four-story apartment building at 47th and Locust Streets were low-income individuals; most of them were Black Americans, though there were also some West Africans. With a tan rug attached to the entire floor, our fourth-floor, two-bedroom apartment had a corner kitchen and bathroom, a living room big enough to accommodate two black couches, a brown coffee table, a TV, and a wooden dining table and chairs. The building had no elevator, so walking up and down the stairs holding Amadou and household items became a job of its own.

We fell behind on our rent payments, so on three separate occasions, the building managers gave my husband an ultimatum to pay the rent or leave. My family was on the verge of homelessness. My husband found a temporary job delivering packages. I used to stand by the apartment window while holding my baby, looking at my husband outside digging out eight to ten inches of snow around our car so he could go to work. After his long days, he returned home exhausted and frustrated by the travels and the little money he made. The last thing he wanted to hear was the loud crying of our son, so I wondered how long we could keep up with our circumstances.

Life began to stabilize for my family starting in March 2003. My husband found a job as a parking attendant near downtown Philadelphia and kept the same job for fifteen years, working from 5:00 a.m. to 1:00 p.m. Thanks to my husband's consistent income, we were able to take care of our family. I found a job as a salesperson at a shoe and handbag store in Sharon Hill, about an hour's commute by public transportation or a twenty-minute drive from Philadelphia. I worked from 10:00 a.m. to 6:00 p.m.

Every morning, I packed Amadou's diaper bag with his milk and food, strapped him on my back, and walked four blocks to the babysitter, a kind woman from Niger, with whom he stayed for the day. To save money, I also packed my lunch and water to take to work. I caught a bus and then a trolley to get to the job. I learned to ask customers, "Hi, how can I help you today? What kind of shoes are you looking for? What size are you looking for?" I organized the shoe shipments around the store, tidied up after customers' visits, paid attention to the browsers to help with any questions, and supported customers with their needs in collaboration with the store managers. My husband picked me up at 6:00 p.m., and we picked up Amadou from the babysitter. Once we got home, I took care of our son and fixed dinner, and my husband and I chatted about our days at work. Amadou started walking up the four flights of steps in our building at ten months old! This meant that my husband and I didn't have to carry our child up and down the steps along with groceries and other essential items. I felt a deep sense of relief for this milestone and cried, as I reflected on the many obligations we were managing and how blessed we were that Amadou could help us even as a baby. Through the eyes of my child, I saw the miracles of God and how they manifested in my life, a glimpse of progress breaking through a mountain of problems. I believed there must be better days for us ahead and that our lives were not supposed to be just about adversity.

My husband and I were blessed with another gift: I became pregnant again. I remembered the voices of the doctors who told me that if I were to get pregnant again, I could die from it. But my own inner voice told me that it was safe for me to get pregnant again, that everything would go well. So I ignored the doctors' and nurses' offers of birth control pills and many other options to either reduce my chances of giving birth or eliminate it completely. I knew that I was meant to have more children and believed that just because I had almost lost my life the first time didn't mean that my later pregnancies would be equally threatening. I wanted to have children while I was young and had the energy to handle their needs. During my second pregnancy, I could sleep most nights but suffered from frequent nausea and occasional vomiting. After six months, I avoided eating, so doctors suggested that I drink vanilla milkshakes to gain weight and maintain the baby's health. I stopped working at seven months to protect my health and that of the baby. I carried the baby full-term and even past the delivery due date.

Once, in July 2004, when I went for my routine checkup at the Hospital of the University of Pennsylvania, the doctors said they would induce my delivery while the baby and I were in good condition. They wanted to perform a cesarean, but I insisted that I would deliver normally since both I and the baby were in good health. I knew that having a cesarean section would handicap me for months, and my family couldn't afford that. My husband and I needed to function at full capacity in order to meet our family responsibilities. So the doctors and nurses set up two childbirth stations, one for a cesarean section and one for a normal delivery. The doctors told me that, at any point of the normal delivery, if they noticed something going wrong, they would switch to the cesarean section. Doctors and nurses surrounded me, as my husband stood near my head, seeing everything that was happening. After about twelve hours of labor, my daughter Aissata came into the world with sweet cries! Twenty-two-month-old Amadou had a sister.

The doctors were amazed that less than two years after I almost died during childbirth, I delivered this baby with no complications. I learned that it's important to let my voice be the loudest in my head, even as I consider feedback from others.

Two days later, baby Aissata and I were discharged from the hospital and returned to our apartment. I started breastfeeding

Aissata soon after her birth. My daughter was much quieter than her brother, and I recovered much more quickly. Four weeks later, I returned to work at the shoe and handbag store. After my husband got off work, he dropped me off at my job and stayed with Aissata and Amadou. At 6:00 p.m., he picked me up from work. We maintained that routine until my daughter was four months old, and then I started taking her to the same babysitter who watched Amadou.

One morning I was packing the children's bags and my own in preparation for the day ahead when I developed a cramp in my back. I couldn't walk, stand, or move around, so I called the shoe store and told them I couldn't come in. I asked my husband to return home as soon as possible to help me with the children. The next day, I went to the hospital and a doctor asked me about any weight that I regularly carry. I told her that every day, from Monday through Friday, I strapped baby Aissata on my back while holding Amadou's hand as we went down the four flights of steps and walked four blocks to the babysitter, one heavy bag in my right hand and the other on my left shoulder. My husband and I still couldn't afford a baby stroller.

Soon after my back spasm, we bought a used stroller at a local flea market for my daughter, and it had space underneath the seat, where I placed our bags as we walked to the babysitter. Our morning walks continued, no matter what the weather was, rainy, snowy, windy, cold. Some days, when it rained or snowed, I was concerned about the impact of the weather on my children. I covered baby Aissata with a plastic rain protector and dressed Amadou in a warm coat, gloves, hat, and water-resistant shoes. Amadou smiled and played in the rain and the snow; my anxieties diminished as I watched his joy and smiled along with him. My son saw rain and snow as moments to play, while I worried; I was glad we had different perspectives. Amadou just needed to be a child and let my husband and me worry about the big questions of our survival as a family.

My employer had two stores. After the birth of my daughter in the summer of 2004, I worked with Mr. Usher, the owner, instead of at his other location, where I had worked with his wife and two teenage sons. Mr. Usher was an immigrant from Armenia, had lived in the United States for many years, and spoke in his native language to his wife and sons.

I continued to improve my English by speaking with customers. I welcomed them to the store and assisted them with their shopping. Many times customers said they were just browsing, but I persuaded them to buy a pair of shoes or a handbag they hadn't even considered.

Many customers had a hard time finding shoes. I would prepare a space for them to sit down, ask them about the shoes they had in mind, look around the store, bring them many options based on their specifications, and help them try on the different choices. Customers often told me, "You must really love your job! You're so helpful and kind." Most of them were Black American women between the ages of twenty and forty. Gradually my English improved to the point where Mr. Usher told me, "Now your English is better than mine!" He liked my interactions with customers and said I did much better with them than he did. He noticed that no matter what the customers' complaints were when they talked to me, we resolved them without arguments.

One day, he started teaching me how to use the cash register, and once I understood how to manage the machine, he left me with that responsibility. A customer, a Black woman in her fifties, was surprised. "He lets you use the cash register?" she said. "I've been coming here for years, and I never saw anybody use that cash register but him and his family. He must really trust you." Mr. Usher started to spend most days in his office at the back of the store and let me manage the customers and the money. When the merchandise shipments arrived, we worked together to organize and display them around the store. He thanked me often for my work and said the fact I dealt well with customers allowed him to have peace of mind and handle other aspects of the business. "You do your work; you take care of your family; everything is good," he said to me often.

One spring morning in 2007, I received shocking news about Mr. Usher. I had left the store after a long day of work, and Mr. Usher and I wished one another good night as he locked up. "See you tomorrow," we said to one another. That was the last time I saw him. He had a heart attack and died in his car on the way home, after pulling into a nearby gas station. The next morning Mr. Usher's youngest son called to tell me the flabbergasting news, which left me in disbelief for days. I was reminded that today is really all we have and that no one has control over what happens tomorrow.

Mr. Usher had told me many times that he didn't want to live so long that he became a burden to his family or society. He didn't want people taking care of him. In many ways that wish was realized, since not a single family member was with him when he died. After Mr. Usher's death, I kept thinking about how short life is and how every encounter with someone could be the last one. My husband and I attended his funeral, and I soon returned to work, but the store was never the same. Mrs. Usher and her younger son told me that they weren't sure they could keep the store open and that their financial situation didn't allow them to pay me. I shared with the family any useful information I knew about managing the store and about Mr. Usher's suppliers. That same spring of 2007, I stopped working in that shoe store.

I soon found another job as a cashier in a neighborhood retail store within walking distance of our home. I worked there until December 2009, when I quit to explore other options for my life. By that point, I had grown in my ability to communicate in English, to sell, and to interact with people across cultures and backgrounds, all of which had enhanced my confidence and had given me a sense that I had unexplored potential.

Chapter Three

The Turning Point

IN JANUARY 2010, I STARTED ON A COMPLETELY DIFFERENT path: I returned to school.

When Amadou and Aissata began attending prekindergarten in 2007, I often volunteered to help in their classrooms. I read to the children; participated in their activities, such as painting and drawing; helped serve them breakfast and lunch and cleaned up afterward; played jump rope with them during recess; and prepared them for nap time. Their classes held "100 book" challenges: parents signed up to read to their kids every day, and if the kids listened to 100 books by the end of the school year, they got a prize. I signed up for Amadou and Aissata, and we started reading nonstop, although I was less interested in the prize and more interested in the kids learning how to read well. I read to them about five books a day, at the library, at home during the day, and at bedtime. We went to our local library at least twice a week to check out and return books. Aissata started reading at three and Amadou at four! We ended up reading more than six hundred children's books!

I carried with me the experiences from my children's prekindergarten classes long after we moved on, especially a rekindled desire to learn and a growing love of teaching. This experience lit in me a desire for knowledge that had been buried beneath life's challenges since I had dropped out of school in Dakar. I went on to become an avid reader.

By the summer of 2009, I had become more confident reading in English and started borrowing memoirs and autobiographies from our local library. I wanted to learn more about the experiences of Black Americans—their perspectives, their struggles, their progress—and to see where I and my family fit within that picture. These are some of the stories that stayed with me.

I read *The Souls of Black Folk,* in which W. E. B. Du Bois wrote about "double consciousness," the idea that Black people in America have evaluated themselves and their lives through the eyes and experiences of White people. Du Bois's book was published in 1903; over a hundred years had elapsed since then, yet his point remained relevant.

I read *I Know Why the Caged Bird Sings* by Maya Angelou. Her life too was defined by racism and discrimination while growing up in the 1930s and '40s in the segregated town of Stamps, Arkansas. I later read Angelou's poem "Still I Rise," which told the story of both the individual and collective abuse that Black Americans had experienced and their progress, as illustrated by Angelou's own story of becoming a prominent writer.

I read *The Autobiography of Martin Luther King, Jr.,* where he painted a detailed picture of the civil rights movement of the 1960s. Hot tears dripped down my face as Dr. King described peaceful Black marchers in Birmingham, Alabama, fighting for the right to vote and be treated as human beings and American citizens, and how they were brutally attacked by White law enforcement with fire hoses, dogs, and clubs. Black people could not share anything with White people. Everywhere they went, there were signs that read "white only" or "colored only." Dr. King refused to settle for these conditions. I also read *A Call to Conscience*, a collection of Dr. King's speeches. Dr. King did everything he could to help Black people regain a sense of dignity and self-respect and had a tremendous impact on improving race relations in America. With every page, I gained a better understanding of racism in America and of the experiences of Black Americans both before and during the 1960s and down to the present day.

I read *The Autobiography of Malcolm X* and *Malcolm Speaks*, a collection of his speeches. Malcolm X's authentic voice as he challenged an oppressive system that defined his life and that of his family stayed with me. He made a clear choice to either live as a free human being in America or die fighting for that freedom. He only went to school up to eighth grade but educated himself in prison and was able to change his life drastically. He was also willing to restart from scratch when necessary, as he did while imprisoned or when he lost his prominent position as a leader in the Nation of Islam after learning more about the Islamic religion through his pilgrimage to Mecca. At thirty-nine years old, in 1965, Malcolm X was murdered in front of his wife and children, fighting for human rights, dignity, freedom, and opportunity for every Black person in America.

I read *Dreams from My Father* by Barack Obama, the son of a Kenyan man and a White American woman. He struggled to find his place in America and to connect with his family in Kenya, and in 2005 he went on to serve as a U.S. senator, only the fifth Black American to do so. His story was that of yearning to belong and achieving against tremendous odds. I met Obama at a rally in our neighborhood in October 2008, when he was a presidential candidate and soon to be the first Black president of the United States. This was a time when the world seemed to revolve around Obama, yet shaking his hand allowed me to experience our shared humanity. If he accomplished extraordinary things, I felt, so could I and any other human being.

These stories and others provided me with a broad and intimate understanding of American society. Each story allowed me to contextualize systemic issues, such as poverty, racism, and inequities in education, employment, and housing, and also revealed the possibilities available to people, regardless of their personal background.

In our neighborhood in West Philadelphia and the shoe store where I worked, many Black Americans used to tell me, "You're a beautiful Black woman." I didn't understand why they would always say "Black woman" instead of only "woman." In Senegal, I was regarded, and regarded myself, simply as a girl, later as a woman, not a "Black girl," a "Black woman." I saw myself through the lens of my humanity, nationality, and ethnicity, not through race or Blackness. I hadn't thought about what my skin color meant for my life.

The books I read and my own experiences living in predominantly Black-populated neighborhoods in West Philadelphia led me to understand that race, especially Blackness, defined people's very existence and their livelihood in society, such as their education, health, job, housing, and safety. Getting this clearer picture of racism in America was critical in my integration into the country.

I had experienced poverty in Senegal and was experiencing it in America, so I wanted to break that cycle. Returning to school was one way I might lift myself and my family out of poverty. I knew that my kids would need my help with their education for years to come. I knew that I was in charge of helping them with their homework. I knew that my English was still insufficient to assist my kids long-term. I knew, too, that our family needed more than one consistent income to sustain us. Though my husband and I did our best to shield our children from our circumstances, our family survived below the poverty line. I wanted a different life for us, one that included enough financial freedom to live, not just survive.

For us, poverty meant a perpetual battle to live. My husband and I were always short on money to manage our day-to-day lives; we always worked in low-paying jobs and struggled to keep up with our bills and access healthcare. Our children didn't attend quality schools and lacked safe places to play outdoors. We used government assistance to buy food and mostly shopped at thrift stores and flea markets for clothes, shoes, and household items, such as furniture and dishes. We lived in a low-income neighborhood, where our lives remained in constant danger of gun violence, and had to stomach ongoing police presence and witness continual clashes between police and residents. We were exposed to nonstop drug dealing, and alcohol was sold in every corner store.

In January 2010, I signed up for a General Education Development program, the GED being the equivalent of a high school diploma in the United States. At that point, Amadou was in first grade and Aissata in kindergarten, and my husband was still clocking in at his job as a parking attendant. He was fully supportive of my returning to school.

My morning classes took place at the School District of Philadelphia's building on Broad Street; my classmates were all like me, adults. The teacher spoke fast and shared tips for taking the different GED tests for math, science, reading, writing, and social studies. She told us where to get books for our studies and how to sign up to take the different GED tests when we were ready. She also suggested simply taking the tests to gauge our levels of mastery, even if we didn't pass. I took her advice, and within three months of completing the GED classes, I started signing up for the tests. I passed the tests for reading, writing, and social studies on the first try but failed science and math. Earning the GED diploma in the state of Pennsylvania required scoring at least 2,250 points total for all five subjects with a minimum score of 410 points per test.

At the GED testing center, I learned about a training program to become a certified nursing assistant in the state of Pennsylvania and thought that job could be a good way to support my family. I enrolled to train as a nurse's aide while simultaneously continuing to take my GED classes. In the mornings, after I had dropped my children off at school, I attended the nurse's aide classes. In the afternoon, my husband picked up the children from school; I returned home to help them with their homework and took them to their after-school activities, fixed dinner, and then went to my evening GED classes.

By the time I completed the nurse's aide training, I had passed four out of the five GED tests but had failed the math test twice. I found a job at a nursing agency in downtown Philadelphia. The GED classes were also taught in the same building that housed the nursing agency, so I continued taking my math lessons there. Every week, I went to classes for two days and worked for three days. I retook my math test for the third time and passed! When I received my GED diploma in the mail, my husband framed it and hung it on our living room wall as a constant reminder of my academic progress. In June 2011, I attended two events celebrating two milestones: my graduation from my GED and nurse's aide programs. My husband and children were there to cheer for me. Amadou shouted in both ceremonies as I walked across the stage to be congratulated, "That's my mom!" The nurse's aide program gave me an outstanding achievement award for earning my GED and nurse's aide certificates at the same time.

The nursing agency placed me with different clients, all of whom were Black women in their seventies or older and suffered from critical health conditions. One of my clients lived by herself in a two-story apartment building. I helped her prepare her three daily meals and take a shower, and I cleaned up her place. Herself, her apartment, and her TV were all that she had.

I worked with another client who lived with her husband and was an amputee from complications related to diabetes. She had tried many different prosthetic legs that failed to accommodate her and finally received a promising one during my time with her. She sat in her wheelchair most of the day; I helped her wash herself, get dressed, put on her prosthetic leg, and practice walking with it. I tidied her bedroom, dusted and vacuumed her house, and prepared a breakfast of eggs, grits, sausage, and coffee for her and her husband. Their children were grown and had moved on with their lives, but one of them lived near their house and checked on them often. I liked working with that couple the most; they were welcoming and appreciated the services I provided to them two to three times a week. They still liked and respected one another after decades of marriage and contentedly entertained themselves with TV game shows like *The Price Is Right* and *Let's Make a Deal*.

One week, I worked with a client twice and called the nursing agency to let them know that I was never returning to that house. That client lived with her son, newly released from prison, in an area of West Philadelphia that seemed abandoned because the majority of the homes there were either damaged or unoccupied. Her son wore an ankle monitor and reported to his probation officer daily. The house was crammed with books, stuffed animals, papers, dishes, clothes, shoes, and furniture. It looked like the client had just moved in and hadn't yet organized anything. She was hooked up to an oxygen tank and sat on her couch watching TV, except when she used her electric wheelchair, attached to a lift, to ride upstairs, where I helped her shower and get dressed. The kitchen was filled with unorganized utensils, pots, and pans, but with difficulty, I managed to prepare some eggs and hot dogs and toast some bread. I felt suffocated and unsafe in that environment, both in the house and outside, and got intense headaches every day after I left.

Every week, I carried around emotional pain and stress connected to the many critically ill women I was helping. I couldn't detach myself from the clients' health struggles and isolating conditions. I couldn't be a pleasant wife or mother in that unhealthy state. So when I stopped working to prepare for the birth of my third child, I never returned to the job. I learned that being a home health aide wasn't for me, so I needed to try something else.

One night in March 2011, I learned that I had lost an important person in my life. Yaye's grandson called to share that Yaye had gotten critically ill and was taken to a hospital but passed away soon after getting there. By that point, I hadn't seen Yaye in almost ten years since I left Dakar and was preparing to visit her that July, but she left this world before I could accomplish that. Over the years, I had grown to truly appreciate Yaye's contributions in my life, especially as I was raising my own children and I began to understand the responsibilities and sacrifices involved. I had maintained regular phone communication with her throughout the years.

The last time we spoke with each other was about two weeks before she passed away. Her death plunged me into profound sorrow, both because I would never see her again and because I had so narrowly missed an opportunity to see her once more before she died. During our last conversation, Yaye prayed for me and my family; she blessed us, leaving us in the hands of God to continue to guide and take care of us. I felt chills all over my body as she spoke; I sensed that she was telling me goodbye. My final words to her were, "Yaye, yen dji de djam," meaning "Yaye, may we see each other in peace." Yaye responded, "Yen dji de djam nenam," meaning "May we see each other again in peace, my child."

Today, Yaye continues to be in my heart and in my mind; she continues to guide me. I still miss her, but I'm comforted that we had prayed for one another, we had blessed one another, we had learned from one another. May Yaye's beautiful heart continue to shine on earth through the blessings she poured into me.

Just as a critical person in my life died, a blessing was born. One late Thursday afternoon in January 2012, when I was full-term with my third pregnancy, I went to my routine checkup at the Hospital of the University of Pennsylvania. The doctors checked me and the baby thoroughly and even ran blood tests and said everything looked fine, so I should go home soon. But a doctor came back shortly after to tell me that they saw a drop in the baby's heartbeat, which meant they had to continue to monitor him and me longer than expected.

She returned later to tell me, "Based on the drop in the baby's heartbeat, we can't let you go home. We're going to send you to the labor floor and start the delivery process." I was in shock! I couldn't believe what she was saying quite yet. So I asked her again, "Do you mean I'm going into labor?" She said yes and added that the baby looked pretty healthy, so they didn't want to take any chances by sending me back home. "I just don't know whether to cry or smile, because I'm not mentally ready yet," I responded. "I understand; I'm going to give you some time to think about it," the doctor said. By then, it was almost 11:00 p.m.

The following day, my husband had to be at work at 5:00 a.m., and the kids didn't have school. I called my husband to share news of the planned delivery and told him to bring the kids to me early in the morning, so he could go to work. He brought the kids to me the next morning and headed to work. I was on the labor floor and under anesthesia but still felt pain from the contractions. My husband's colleague replaced him at work, so he rushed back to the hospital at around 9:30 a.m., took the kids to stay with them, and returned with them to stick around until 5:00 p.m. when a doctor said I wasn't yet ready for delivery. She would monitor my progress for two more hours and then decide whether to perform a cesarean section, which I very much wanted to avoid.

Thankfully, I ended up having a normal delivery. I called my husband to come back to the hospital with the kids, who were supervised by a nurse outside of the room where I was delivering my baby. I didn't want my children to witness my agonizing pain or the delivery. My husband held my hand throughout the delivery as nurses and doctors surrounded me. At around close to 8:00 p.m., baby Ibra made his grand entrance into the world with beautiful cries! My husband, kids, and I were very happy to see and hold Ibra. I started breastfeeding him minutes after his birth and was discharged from the hospital two days later.

With the birth of my first child, I learned just how isolated and lonely my husband and I were and that people we thought we could count on would not be there for us because we were not worth their time and effort. With the birth of my second child, I learned to keep faith alive because no matter how bad the situation looks, things could always turn out for the better. With the birth of my third child, I felt whole and a sense of inner peace. I had gained confidence in myself as a parent, no longer grieved over our lack of external help, and made most decisions based on what I could personally handle and what my husband could support me in. My faith in God, myself, and the possibilities in life had grown over the years. I believed that my destiny was in no one else's hands but God's and that everything that was meant for me in my lifetime would happen.

I soon embarked on a journey totally unfamiliar to me; I decided to attend college. For years, my family and I were surviving paycheck to paycheck, squeezed by financial constraints, and I wanted that to change. I no longer wanted a mere job but a career that would sustain me and my family long-term and provide us with the financial freedom to live more fully and with less stress. I thought attending college could offer me more options to pursue a career. I also wanted to continue to improve my academic skills, so I could support my children in their ongoing education.

One day in the summer of 2012, I tied baby Ibra on my back and visited the same family friend who had previously babysat Amadou and Aissata. I told her about my plans to attend the Community College of Philadelphia (CCP) for the upcoming school year and asked if she could watch my baby boy when I started classes, and she agreed to do so. By then, Amadou was ten years old, Aissata nine, and Ibra five months.

I was a first-generation college student—that is the first in my family to attend college—and the only married woman I knew of in the Senegalese immigrant community in West Philadelphia who was attending college. The majority of Senegalese women in my community were hair braiders, and the majority of the Senegalese men were businessmen or worked as parking attendants or taxi drivers. I started my enrollment process at CCP having no clue about the time commitment or the academic and financial demands of college life.

My CCP enrollment process involved five steps. I completed an admission application, applied for federal financial aid, activated my student account, took a placement test, and finally registered for my reading and writing courses. To complete these processes, I had to go back and forth between two different CCP campuses with Ibra tied on my back or sitting in his stroller while I talked to financial and academic advisors and figured out federal financial aid. While I zigzagged from office to office, person to person, people often stopped me on the streets and campuses to greet Ibra and chat with him. "He's so cute! How old is your baby? He is the cutest little thing!" Ibra would smile and flash his bright eyes at the people interacting with him. At times, I found quiet places on campus, covered Ibra in a blanket, breastfed him, and then walked to the next office for the next round of paperwork and decision-making.

The direction of my life began to change from this point on, though at first, I didn't see what the new direction would be. My first concern was not selecting a major or a career but simply how I would get through the first weeks and semester of my studies. I knew that if I could complete the first semester of college, I could build on that momentum to continue. In the fall of 2012, I didn't know what to expect, but I was eager to learn and knew that I especially needed to improve my English and math skills. I prioritized fulfilling my family responsibilities, remediating my academic weaknesses, and looking for financial aid.

I was taking a "leap of faith" on education and had no idea how it would turn out. I feared that I could once again fail as I had before. But there was a louder voice in my head that said that this time was different. I was going to school not just to get an education but also to better help my kids with their studies and further their intellectual growth. I was going to school because my family and I needed a better financial situation. I had a much deeper desire to learn than my teenage self had had. This time, my education could make a difference in my life and that of my family.

Ms. Shashaty was my first college professor. She combined expertise, seriousness, and clarity in her teaching. I took two remedial English courses with her, one focused on reading comprehension and one on writing and grammar. I told her toward the beginning of the semester to bear with me throughout the course because I was learning English and still needed a lot of practice to improve my writing skills. Most days that semester, I attended classes with excruciating pain in my chest from not breastfeeding Ibra during the long hours I was in school. My entire chest felt like someone was poking needles into it. I didn't tell Ms. Shashaty or other classmates but simply did my best to get through each class, hoping that eventually the pain would stop.

I had another serious academic weakness. I couldn't type on a word processor and didn't know how to learn to do so. When Ms. Shashaty first assigned us an essay to write, I worried that it could be the end of my college career. I asked an academic advisor if CCP offered any typing classes because I didn't know how to type and many of the assignments required typed papers. The adviser said that the college didn't offer a typing class, but many students struggled with a similar problem and were able to get through their classes. Her answer didn't provide a solution to my problem, but at least I knew I wasn't alone and could maybe get through my classes without knowing how to type.

I first handwrote my papers in notebooks, had them checked by English tutors, and edited them. Then, I would spend all day at the college's computer lab typing them, then hours editing them with different tutors, and then more hours back at a computer incorporating those edits. My eyes watered with tears of disappointment and frustration when I first typed an essay because of how excruciatingly slow I was. I wondered, *How could I get through college at this rate?* But I persisted anyway. I sat in the front of every class to minimize distractions, took notes, participated in discussions, asked the professor questions, and completed all my assignments on time.

Outside of class, I squeezed learning into my life's routine. Before class, I dropped Amadou and Aissata off at school, prepared Ibra and his diaper bag with all his needs, took him to the babysitter at around 11:15 a.m., and then went to CCP for my classes. My husband picked up Amadou and Aissata from school, made sure they ate lunch, and stayed with them until I got home. After I left CCP, I picked up Ibra from the babysitter, breastfed him, helped his siblings with homework, took them to their after-school activities and brought them back, fixed dinner for the family, and then stayed up until midnight or later completing my assignments. I did my schoolwork while breastfeeding Ibra, while carrying him on my back, or while he was asleep. I took all of my class materials with me to the after-school activities of Amadou and Aissata and did my work while the kids swam, played basketball, or practiced karate at our local YMCA. I was always on the clock, doing something related to family or school; I only had time to myself when I went to bed.

I learned how to read texts critically and to annotate, summarize, paraphrase, and respond to them. One skill that I really enjoyed learning from Ms. Shashaty was annotating a text, and I applied the method to all of my readings because it allowed me to get intimate with written words and their writers and to gain a deep understanding of the materials I read. While reading texts, I used a pencil to underline the most important sentences in each paragraph and drew star symbols next to them to show their importance. I summarized each paragraph or page I read in one or two sentences in the margins of the texts. I circled words I didn't understand and looked them up in a dictionary. I also circled the names of people who were featured in the text to keep track of the information given about each one. In a separate notebook, I compiled vocabulary words that I would later look up and write sentences for. I reacted to the texts as I read by drawing smiley faces or sad faces to show how I felt about the information. I wrote a question mark next to passages I didn't understand and an exclamation point near something exciting or dramatic. I asked questions on the margins, almost as if I were talking to someone, maybe the author. I wrote "agree" or "disagree" next to a paragraph or sentence I felt strongly about and connected my readings to my personal experiences. I read aloud to myself for about ten minutes every day to practice pronouncing words and sentences. I listened to the words I struggled with, using an online dictionary and rereading them aloud over and over until I got comfortable saying them. By the time I needed to summarize, paraphrase, or respond to the texts, I was prepared for such assignments. I also worked continually with English tutors to help me edit my papers.

Ms. Vicky was one of those English tutors who poured so much of their time and knowledge into me. She edited, corrected, and explained the errors in my grammar, spelling, punctuation, sentence structure, and word choice. The combination of Ms. Vicky's one-on-one, patient English tutoring style and the ongoing questions I asked her to better understand her edits and avoid repeating them for the next paper allowed me to improve my writing skills with each session. I thought that I was making only slow progress, but looking back I see that, given the many writing skills that I needed to improve on, my learning process was relatively fast, and that was because of the support I got from Ms. Vicky and other English tutors as well as my own commitment to improve.

I went to the Learning Lab for tutoring at least ten hours a week throughout that semester, and outside of school, I spent another ten to thirty hours a week practicing my writing and reading skills in some capacity, whether it was looking up words and writing down their meanings, taking online grammar quizzes, annotating texts, or reading aloud to my children. Learning academic English became part of my daily routine. I was so grateful to Ms. Vicky that I wrote her a thank-you note for her efforts in supporting my learning. My English learning experiences that first semester opened my eyes to my potential as a student and trained me to become better at juggling marriage, motherhood, and education.

At the end of the semester, I met with Ms. Shashaty for her overall feedback about my learning progress and to get my final grades for her two courses. In one class, I finished with 94 out of 100, and in another class with 96 out of 100. Since these courses were pass/fail, my scores would not show up in my academic record, but Ms. Shashaty told me that students in remedial classes generally didn't score as high as I had and added, "Aminata, you have what it takes to get your master's degree." I was so puzzled by her statement that I wrote it down to reflect on. I remember thinking, "How do I have what it takes to get a master's degree? I'm an English learner, just wrapping up remedial classes I had to take because my English skills were not adequate for college-level work." But just as a part of me questioned her assessment of my academic abilities, another part of me believed her. Ms. Shashaty knew her subject matter well and had also gotten to know me as a student. I handed Ms. Shashaty a thank-you note and told her how much I appreciated learning from her. I kept her words about the master's degree somewhere in my mind, but it seemed unattainable to me. Instead, I focused only on signing up for classes for the following semester, while still worrying about how to balance my home and school lives.

That day, I went home and talked to my baby, Ibra, who was ten months old, as I wept tears of joy. "Thank you, my baby, for letting me learn. Thank you for being a good baby to your mommy. I finished my first semester with good grades! May God bless you and always protect you! I love you, baby!" I gave Ibra so many kisses and hugs for helping me in my college education by accepting the babysitter and bottle-feeding; if he hadn't, I would have dropped my studies. Throughout my time in school that semester, I felt Ibra's absence and wanted to be with him. The piercing pain in my chest for not breastfeeding him remained a constant reminder that I was away from my baby for many hours. But I suppressed those feelings so I could focus on my learning and then gave Ibra my full attention when I returned home.

Ibra had cried and thrown tantrums for about two weeks, and then he started to embrace his new routine of being away from me for hours at a time and of being bottle-fed with baby formula. Those were big changes for him and for me, and we didn't know how they would impact us or if we could sustain them for months. Without having a clue as to what was happening, Ibra helped me start and continue my college education. Ibra loved to stay with me and to breastfeed as much as he wanted, cuddle up in my arms or be tied on my back, sit leaning back against my chest while I read aloud to him story after story, or stroll around through our West Philadelphia neighborhood on our way to our local library or the YMCA.

The following semester, in the spring of 2013, I enrolled in two college-level English classes and a remedial math course. My English professor was Ms. Ravyn, a dynamic and passionate woman who taught with confidence and conviction. In her classes, I dove deeper into reading literature and writing essays. I liked hearing Ms. Ravyn read aloud from our different texts and how she had students, including me, also read to the class. I liked her passion for teaching; I felt her love for literature and her desire to see her students perform well in her classes. I went to her office hours almost every week to ask questions about assignments and to have her critique my papers as I was in the process of writing them. She gave clear feedback and edits that allowed me to improve my essays week after week.

Her paper assignments covered a range of social issues in the United States, such as inequities in education from kindergarten through college, immigrant experiences in the K–12 grades, racism, classism, toxic masculinity, and media depiction of women. Thinking and writing about these social issues increased my desire to engage and be a part of the solution, especially when it came to education. I grew to enjoy the process of coming up with an idea for an essay, writing about it, getting feedback and editing support to improve it, and finalizing my work for submission. I became appreciative of the writing process that I had dreaded in my two previous English classes because I started to see how it helped to clarify my thoughts and even shape my actions. I became faster at editing and typing my papers. Ms. Ravyn would later write a scholarship recommendation letter on my behalf that brought me to tears of appreciation for the growth that I experienced in her classes and how she recognized that growth. Below is an excerpt of the letter.

> When I claim that Aminata stood out from her peers on the first day of class, I am not saying so lightly. I was pleasantly surprised by her level of commitment and alert attitude during our first three-hour session. Her energy and sharpness simply did not flag. In the subsequent months as I was getting to know her, I never witnessed a moment when she wasn't energetic, focused, and positive. I am describing these aspects of her personality to impress upon you what I think makes Aminata such a success no matter what she attempts—she knows how to learn, and she exemplifies how resilience and persistence yield great results. If you couple her personality with her organizational skills and her work ethic, you will see a portrait of a student who will be able to do great things in all manner of rigorous academics.

Ms. Ravyn's letter reminded me of the many hours that I had spent thinking and working through different essay topics, meeting with her and tutors for support, and editing at least ten drafts for each assignment. I discovered in her class that I loved writing and wanted to continue to improve. Her class papers became less about completing those final drafts and getting good grades and more about the actual writing process and the intellectual exploration of social issues that millions across the United States, including myself, dealt with. That's why I set a personal standard of excellence for the papers because I genuinely cared about the issues that I wrote about and wanted to discuss them as clearly as possible. I was beginning to realize that I loved learning languages for their own sake. As a child, I had to learn several different languages to communicate with the important people in my life—Pulaar, Wolof, French—so learning a fourth language, English, did not seem like an impossible undertaking. In addition, I took three consecutive Spanish courses at CCP and as a tutor, passed on what I knew about the language to my peers.

Throughout my academic career, I met professors, instructors, tutors, advisors, administrators, and students who were willing to support me in my efforts to improve and get to the next level. I believe that once you take full ownership of your academic career, you'll attract people who can guide you in achieving, even surpassing, your goals. Pursuing anything worthwhile can feel and be lonely; however, if you open your mind and heart to getting support, people will help you improve beyond your expectations.

In the spring of 2013, I also took my first math class at CCP, with Mr. Reading, an energetic professor. During our first day of class, he asked students to introduce themselves to the class. When it was my turn to speak, I said that I had never liked math and struggled with it throughout my schooling and ended with "I'm ready to learn, and I'm happy to be here." Mr. Reading listened and smiled, told me that I was in the right place, and welcomed me to the class. That was the lowest-level remedial math class that the college offered; it taught arithmetic—adding, subtracting, multiplying, and dividing—and was designed for students like me, who were relearning the basics. The class had its special book from which Mr. Reading assigned homework after every session. When he assigned us twenty problems, I did forty of them or even more, until I felt confident with the concepts. I was relearning arithmetic, because I had been out of school for over a decade, and I had forgotten how to do it.

I decided that memorizing the times tables would help me solve many of the math problems. Every day, I committed to writing the times tables from two to twelve in a composition book. I scored in the nineties for the first two math assignments and 100 in the third one! That day, I called my husband over our class break to share the news of my grade, and Mr. Reading's reaction to it. I told my husband that I couldn't believe that I scored a hundred in math, given all of my shortcomings with the subject and that Mr. Reading took about fifteen minutes of class time praising my work. He began by saying that he didn't mention individual students' grades in his classes but had to speak up on mine. He became teary-eyed with pride as he reminded me that I had admitted my weakness in math but had constantly put in the work and had improved in a relatively short amount of time. He added, "You are the reason I teach. Students like you are the reason I teach." I felt both honored and put on the spot. I simply wanted to improve my learning; I didn't want to be highlighted for doing so. Many students congratulated me during our break. The hours of practicing math and doing the homework paid off, and I continued to maintain high scores in Mr. Reading's class until I completed the course—me, the woman who didn't know her times tables a few months earlier! If you don't give up, anything is possible.

I knew from that class that math would no longer be a barrier to my education, though it would continue to be a challenge. I had memorized my times tables and could add, subtract, multiply, and divide with confidence. I asked the professor and tutors clarifying questions regarding specific math problems that I struggled with, practiced problems until I felt confident I understood them well, and sought out tutoring support throughout the semester. I knew that I had found a learning system for math that worked and that I could apply it in the upcoming higher-level courses on the subject. As in my other classes, I gained more confidence in dealing with academic challenges and overcoming them through practice and a genuine interest in learning and improving my skills.

My academic progress at community college paid off in other ways as well. I went on to win a scholarship that covered my tuition, books, and fees throughout the remainder of my time at the school, and I was selected for a few more scholarships connected to my academic achievement. I felt a great sense of relief that I could learn without constantly worrying about how I would pay for my education. With my husband's encouragement, I also decided to major in international studies after completing my first year at the school with the intention of hopefully pursuing a career in U.S. diplomacy one day.

It was in the spring of 2014 when I took a class at CCP that made my entire body tremble and my mind race: public speaking. I had the choice of taking a creative writing course or public speaking. I decided to take public speaking because that's the class that terrified me, and I wanted to overcome that fear. In the Senegalese culture in which I grew up, looking directly into people's eyes, especially adults, was considered a sign of disrespect. In American culture, looking away or looking down when talking to people is a sign of not being trustworthy and confident. I wanted to get comfortable speaking in front of people while making eye contact with them as much as possible.

In that course, I wrote and delivered six speeches based on my own experience, research, and the principles of effective public speaking that we learned in class. Students, about twenty of us, were graded in real time as we delivered our speeches; we got written feedback from our peers and the instructor, focusing on content as well as vocal and nonverbal deliveries. During our first session, the professor said, "In this class, you will sink or swim."

My speeches covered key life lessons from Marian Wright Edelman, an activist for civil rights and children's rights; celebrated my aunt Yaye; shared an aspect of Senegalese culture by demonstrating how women tied babies on their backs; addressed racism and race relations in America; and proposed recommendations for the African continent and its youth. As I delivered my speeches, I decided to swim and not sink, though my hands and voice trembled, my body rocked back and forth, and my eyes barely saw the audience. Many peers pointed out that I looked down often and that at times I spoke too fast. But overall, the students wrote that my delivery was clear and memorable and the content purposeful and inspiring.

With every speech, I became a little less nervous, looked at the audience a little more, and read my notes a little less, but delivering the speeches never felt easy, even with all of my preparations. My peers and professor had a different perspective than I did; they focused on the progress that I had been making over time, especially in my level of confidence.

Our fourth assignment involved selecting a speech by someone else and delivering that to the class within a time limit. I chose a commencement address by Marian Wright Edelman, delivered at Lewis & Clark College on May 10, 2014, in which she talked about ten life lessons. I selected six of them: (1) to know that nothing is free, (2) to assign yourself something to do, (3) to never work just for money, (4) to not be afraid to take risks or be criticized, (5) to listen to yourself, and (6) to never give up. After I delivered that speech, one student wrote for his feedback, "I don't think I've ever said this about anyone before, but you're going places. Run for president; I would vote for you." Another student wrote, "You really made this speech yours. For a minute, I thought you were that speaker." I maintained an A grade throughout that course, scoring from ninety to ninety-nine for my various speeches. More than anything, I was proud of challenging myself to speak to an audience despite my fears and to do my best to learn and to share with peers an authentic part of who I was. Sometimes, our best learning experiences come from situations that scare us, but when we embrace them, we meet a more confident version of ourselves on the other side.

Our final speech assignment was to project ourselves into the future and see ourselves as professionals delivering a message to a relevant audience. I spoke as the U.S. assistant secretary of state for African affairs, delivering a speech to the United Nations General Assembly on improving the economic conditions of Africa, especially of its children. I imagined that all of my classmates were heads of state and that the professor was the United Nations Secretary-General Ban Ki-moon.

My speech connected my story to that of other African girls and focused on Senegal. I talked about the need to educate children, especially girls. I proposed three recommendations for the African continent: to invest in the education of African children, to protect and preserve the continent's natural resources, and to address climate change and pollution leading to droughts and food insecurity. The professor wrote for his feedback, "I love the humanitarian purpose of your speech and your excellent knowledge of the topic. It was a wonderful capstone to the semester." A student shared, "I really enjoyed your speeches all semester long. They were very beneficial to us or other audiences you are referring to."

I had willingly signed up for a course that terrified me, one in which I could have truly embarrassed myself publicly because there was nowhere to hide. Up to that point, I had never delivered a speech to any group of people, large or small, and didn't know how the semester would go. Still, I approached the public-speaking course as I had approached the others, by counting on careful preparation to make up for whatever deficits I might have, as well as for my anxiety. I asked the professor questions inside and outside of class in order to better understand his expectations; I wrote, rewrote, and edited my speeches and practiced them in front of tutors, my daughter, and the mirror. By the time I stood in front of the class to speak, I had reduced my anxiety by half. I still trembled and still doubted myself, but I was also confident that I could lean on my preparation even if I forgot my speech. The public speaking class solidified my level of confidence in what I could accomplish once I decided to go for something. In many ways, my fear of speaking in front of people was more about a mental barrier that I needed to push through; it had nothing to do with whether I was capable of delivering speeches. This was true for the bigger challenges in my life as well. I came to accept that how far I could reach depended on my beliefs about myself, even if all odds were against me.

In March of 2015, I experienced another major milestone, an acceptance letter from the University of Pennsylvania! "On behalf of the Admission Committee, it is my pleasure to offer you admission to the Bachelor of Arts in LPS at the College of Professional and Liberal Studies for Fall 2015. Your commitment to personal excellence makes you stand out as someone who will thrive at Penn and make a solid contribution to our community. We believe that you and Penn are very well matched for each other."

CCP wanted to recognize and highlight this achievement to encourage other students, so its communications team organized a photo shoot and an interview with two local publications: *PhillyVoice* and the *Philadelphia Inquirer*. Their reporters interviewed me along with three other CCP students who were also transferring to Penn in the fall of 2015. I told reporters about my plans to study international relations at Penn and my hopes to work in U.S. diplomacy and to contribute to improving education and youth employment in Senegal. I said, "What I took away from this experience is that my voice matters, that I can accomplish anything I want to...I'm not afraid of anything anymore."

I echoed those thoughts in an article published in CCP's student newspaper, the *Vanguard,* on November 26, 2014, titled "Thank you CCP." In the piece, I thanked professors, advisors, tutors, scholarship staff, the *Vanguard* team, and my husband and children, all of whom helped during my time at the college. I talked about the many academic and personal struggles that I dealt with and my dramatic improvement. I wrote, "Today, I am a totally different student. I am confident and believe that I can achieve any level of academic success when I put my mind to it. CCP has shown me that my potentials are limitless as long as I am not afraid to tap into them."

I'm telling you of these achievements to show you what *you* are capable of if you focus and work hard. What I accomplished, you can too. I started out by learning many basics in academic English, such as grammar, vocabulary, punctuation, and pronunciation, and persisted with the process consistently, which eventually led to concrete progress. Whatever you put your mind to, you can achieve.

I don't mean to imply that hard work and belief in yourself are all that you need to achieve your goals. You must also be willing to make sacrifices. Returning to school, especially as an adult with different responsibilities, could cost you more than you imagine. That's why so many people quit. You have to be willing to commit yourself to being a student and give up activities that interfere with that commitment.

I took full ownership of my learning by making it a top priority in my life. This meant any activity I engaged in at the time revolved around my marriage, children, or school. I cut out social activities, such as attending the childbirth or marriage ceremonies that took place frequently in my immigrant community. I stopped watching TV, only occasionally paying attention to the news; I didn't use social media. I picked up phone calls from family members in Senegal only during the weekends. I focused on my education by weaving it into my day-to-day life, such as studying while waiting for my children during their after-school activities. Given the many academic weaknesses I needed to work on while juggling family responsibilities, I still doubted if I could make the necessary progress in my education. But I didn't have the choice of giving up any of my responsibilities; my only choice was to figure out how to fit education into my life as it was.

Many people I knew, both close and far away, misunderstood me; many distanced themselves from me because they couldn't grasp what I was trying to achieve. So part of what I had signed up for when I returned to school was being misunderstood, isolated, and lonely while navigating experiences that were completely new to me. What I did in returning to school was just try. I tried without knowing what I was doing. I tried with some support and learned along the way. I tried with zero guarantee that I would finish the first semester, let alone graduate. I tried in confusion, frustration, tears, fatigue, and isolation. Just try and see what happens.

I failed many times in school growing up, not because I was incapable of learning but because I lacked the necessary support system. Those failures, my separation from my parents, and my childhood trauma bruised my self-esteem and belief in my capabilities. What I learned, though, is that we must distinguish between what happens to us in our lives and what we choose to do with our experiences. Those are two different things. We always have the choice and power to define what our life experiences mean to us. I chose to give school another shot, and it worked. I hope you'll always choose to bet on yourself even if all the odds are against you. What meaning do you want to give to your most difficult life experiences? You have control over your mind and attitude; use them to unlock a sea of possibilities.

Graduation day marked the end of one academic experience and the beginning of another. On the morning of May 2, 2015, I graduated with the highest honors among more than 2,000 CCP students and was only one of three people to earn an associate's degree in international studies. My family and I shared the joyous occasion; I felt so much gratitude for both the struggle and the progress.

Chapter Four

Juggling Identities

THAT MONDAY IN JULY 2011 HAD STARTED OUT ALMOST like any other summer day, but it was a unique one for me, because at the end of it, at around 10:40 p.m., my family and I were waiting to board a Turkish Airlines flight from John F. Kennedy International Airport in New York City. Our destination: Dakar, Senegal. Once on board the plane and about two hours into the flight, my husband and children started to fall asleep, but my eyes remained wide open. Excited and anxious, I wanted to take in all of the experiences of this trip. After ten years in America, I was returning to Senegal. I looked forward to reconnecting with Senegalese culture by revisiting the people and scenes of my childhood and teenage years. However, once I arrived in Dakar, I realized how American society had changed me because I felt like a stranger in my home country. I had changed, the situations in my life had changed, and Senegal had changed. My idea of "home" didn't match reality.

I left Senegal as a twenty-one-year-old newly married woman. I had previously lived with my aunt, Yaye, who raised me. I liked many aspects of Senegalese social life; there was always a celebration or event of some sort going on. A relative, friend, or neighbor would be getting married or giving birth, for example, or relatives would spend a day just visiting us. I too would visit family members often. Senegal had felt warm and welcoming; its people cared about one another. When the family and I were having a meal together, neighbors would randomly walk into the house, and we would make space for them to eat with us.

Most importantly, my Aunt Yaye was there. As I was growing up, Yaye didn't just teach me good values by lecturing; she embodied and demonstrated them to me every day. When family members were sick, she visited and comforted them. When family members were getting married, she went to congratulate them. When family members gave birth, she gave their newborns massages every day for at least a month. She knew all of her relatives well. She was the definition of selflessness and generosity and embodied every aspect of what it meant to be a Senegalese and a kind human being. Some of the most important values I learned from her were perseverance, patience, generosity, and resilience, all of which would serve me long after I left Dakar.

When I arrived in Dakar, at first I was just happy to reunite with my mom after being separated for twenty-one years and to see relatives. But after the first night, I realized that my desire to visit Senegal was also my desire to see Yaye, who had passed away a few months before I came. I felt the emptiness that she left behind. Even though I knew that I would not see her, I didn't fully grasp the impact her passing would have on me. Only when I went to say goodbye to her at her grave did I truly believe that she was gone forever.

In addition, I realized that I had become impatient with all the various events—the ceremonies of marriage and childbirth, the family get-togethers—that I used to enjoy but now found to be a waste of my time. I didn't like constantly being around people as I used to before moving to America. I now enjoyed having quiet time to myself to read, write, think, or just take a nap. I had grown accustomed to a structured life; therefore, I didn't tolerate all the unpredictable events that occurred on any given day. For instance, sometimes I would plan to go to the beach with my kids, but it would wind up not happening because anywhere from one to four relatives came to visit my family unannounced. In America, on the other hand, my life had an established daily routine around my children's schooling and my own, their afterschool activities, and our family time. All of the activities ran like clockwork, day in and day out until I went to bed. It was challenging to go all of a sudden from such a structured life to a lifestyle with little to no structure at all.

I also sensed how relatives treated me differently now because I came from America. They had high financial expectations of me. I felt that my relationship with my relatives would never be as genuine as it was before I immigrated to America because almost everyone expected money or a gift from me. That left me feeling like a stranger in my own family and reduced the level of comfort and ease that I used to have with my relatives. I had to accept the hard truth that when I left Senegal in 2001, in a sense I left it for good and would never really be able to come back home again.

My trip to Senegal also gave me closure in many ways. I accepted that Yaye had passed away and that I would never see her again. I accepted that my relationship with my mom would never be the same because our roles had changed—I took charge of supporting her livelihood; my dad had passed years prior.

Separating from my parents at ten years old has meant eternally broken bonds. My mom, dad, and brother moved to Senegal from the Democratic Republic of Congo soon after I immigrated to America in 2001. My dad passed away in 2002, and my brother would be buried near his grave two decades later. The distance between me and my mom has remained, with our relationship centered around me helping her live her life with dignity. The time and experiences that we lost with one another and as a family would never be made up. I had learned to bottle up my feelings over the years of separation in which my parents and I barely had even phone conversations. I chose to forgive my parents, so I could live my life and be a parent to my children; I didn't want to pass on any of my childhood pain to my kids.

As I sat on the plane on my way back to America, I felt mixed emotions. I valued experiencing Senegal again and reliving many of my memories growing up there, and I was grateful that I had evolved as a human being from my experiences in America, from marriage, and from motherhood. However, I was profoundly grieved that Yaye was gone. I now understood what it meant to lose someone I admired. I sat in that plane wishing to see, hear, and hold Yaye just one more time and to tell her how much I really cherished her. But I was also grateful that I had listened to Yaye and followed her guidance growing up and had never missed an opportunity during our phone conversations to tell her how much I treasured her. And finally, I was sad that I would no longer be fully comfortable in the place that I had once called "home."

Just as I accepted losing my Senegalese life, I welcomed my new identity as an American. On a spring afternoon in May 2013, I went from a legal permanent resident in America to a U.S. citizen. I knew that I was entering a different phase of my life as an immigrant to America. My family and I went to the United States Citizenship and Immigration Services building in Center City, Philadelphia, to take my oath of allegiance and receive my U.S. naturalization certificate. There were forty-four of us taking this oath that day, representing forty different countries in Africa, Asia, and Europe. I was the only one from Senegal in that group. An administrator sat in front of the room as we walked up to her one at a time to verify that the information on our naturalization certificates was accurate and to hand our green cards and appointment letters to an immigration officer.

On one side of the podium was the light blue and white flag of the U.S. Department of Homeland Security and on the other side, the red, white, and blue flag of America. Some people taking the oath didn't speak English, so an immigration officer struggled to guide them through the proceedings. We each received two booklets, *The Citizen's Almanac* and *The Declaration of Independence of the United States,* along with a small American flag. The moment that I had anticipated for years had finally arrived. Feeling gratitude and enthusiasm, I sat in the front row while my family sat at the back of the room. And from time to time, I heard Ibra scream and my husband trying to calm him down. We watched a video in which Madeleine

Albright talked about immigrating to America from Czechoslovakia with her refugee family as a child and going on to become the first woman to serve as U.S. secretary of state. She encouraged us to apply for a U.S. passport right away. We watched another video titled "Faces of America," which showed people from around the world who had become U.S. citizens. We sang the U.S. national anthem, "The Star-Spangled Banner"; we listened to a performance of "God Bless America"; and we took the oath of allegiance. President Obama congratulated us in a video and welcomed us as full participants in American society. I received my U.S. naturalization certificate! My children didn't really understand the importance of this ceremony, but like me, my husband knew that something had forever changed in my life. I had become a citizen of the United States of America—a country summed up in one word in my experiences and the experiences of millions of immigrants: opportunity.

Opportunity and consistent hard work led me to the University of Pennsylvania, commonly known as Penn. It was one of the best and most selective universities in America and the world, so getting into Penn wasn't just an achievement but could change the trajectory of my life for the better. But after the joy over my admission settled, I asked myself how I was going to pay for my studies. The answer to that question would determine whether I could attend Penn or not. I researched the scholarships available for the College of Liberal and Professional Studies, applied for them, and met with the program's director to discuss potential financial aid. My message, repeated on my written application for a scholarship, was clear: I didn't have the money to pay for a Penn education, so without financial support, I couldn't attend the university. I was living below the poverty line, and if I were indebted by student loans, I would not be able to support my children as much as I should in their educational endeavors. I couldn't sign myself up to pay for my student loans long-term and also help pay for my children's education once they started college.

By then, the spring of 2015, I was in my last semester at Community College of Philadelphia (CCP) and had also been accepted at Temple University with a scholarship offer. However, my first choice was Penn. I wanted to study at a place that challenged me intellectually at the highest level and provided opportunities that would propel me into a potential career in international affairs.

I soon received news from Penn that the school could cover my full tuition and fees as a part-time student until I graduated if I fulfilled the scholarship's requirements, which included enrolling in two courses every semester and maintaining at least a 3.0 grade point average, equivalent to earning at least a B in each course. For about a month and a half in the summer of 2015, I spent six to eight hours per day at the CCP campus in West Philadelphia scanning my courses' syllabi one page at a time and then emailing each one of the documents to at least two or three different Penn programs, asking if they would allow transfer credit for those classes. Some Penn programs accepted the CCP courses as equivalent to their own, some rejected them, and some asked me to send them graded papers in those classes.

My first reaction was, Didn't the university already have everything it needed to evaluate my academic record? Why create a sense of doubt in a student who was already admitted? I had graduated from CCP with the highest honors, earning all As in my courses, and had already provided to Penn my official CCP transcript and syllabi from my courses. Now, I also had to submit graded papers as proof of my academic ability and past performance? I wondered, How did Penn generally deal with transfer students? I didn't think doubting a student was a good way of welcoming that learner to the university, especially after that student had endured many sacrifices to get to that point. Nevertheless, I provided the graded papers as requested, brushed off the experience, and moved on. I went to Penn believing that I could achieve anything that I put my mind to and no one or nothing was going to shake that belief.

Entering Penn, I had a vision for my time there but maintained an open mind for how the experience could actually unfold. I decided to major in international relations with a concentration in African studies, and later I added a minor in English. I set three overall intentions for my time at the university:

- I wanted to learn about the key issues that kept the African continent and its population in perpetual economic crisis and in the process find a way to contribute to the continent's progress
- I hoped to identify the type of diplomatic work that interested me and to get some hands-on experience of it
- I wished to discover new and untapped potentials in myself

Penn and CCP were two different worlds. I started my studies at CCP's West Philadelphia campus, which consisted of one building and continued at the college's main campus, which had seven, clustered near one another. Across its four campuses, over 30,000 students were enrolled at CCP, most of them from Black working-class families.

By contrast, Penn's campus stretched for blocks, with more than 180 buildings and twelve schools, enrolling about 25,000 students, most of them from White upper-class families. I read an estimated one to ten pages for every meeting of a class at CCP, while at Penn I read at least fifty to a hundred per class. Tutoring support was more available to students at CCP than at Penn. I wondered, Could I handle Penn's academic workload? During my first week on campus, I got an answer to that question. I had signed up for two classes in African studies, one anthropology class called Youth and Democracy in Africa and a history class called Introduction to Africa.

The Youth and Democracy in Africa' class was held on Mondays and Wednesdays from 3:30 p.m. to 5:00 p.m. and was attended by six students, including me. On the first day of the class, in August 2015, we, the students and professor, introduced ourselves and discussed the course syllabus and assignments for the semester. Our weekly assignment was to write a summary, no more than a paragraph long, of the key argument in each of the readings for that week and to draft one discussion question per reading that required critical thinking. For the second meeting of this class, I submitted summaries for seven readings, raised one discussion question for each, and turned in my work on time. The topic that week was, What is democracy? Below are two of my write-ups for that week.

> In "Democracy's Lack," Wendy Brown criticizes Habermas's belief that nationalism and capitalism are the ingredients mostly needed in order to have a strong democracy. Instead, Brown insists that democracy has no clear guiding principles, and that citizens of a democratic system usually have no sense of connection with each other. What would a democracy that Brown is satisfied with look like?

> In "From the History of Colonial Anthropology to the Anthropology of Western Hegemony," Talal Asad criticizes anthropological studies for boosting European power during the colonial period because the knowledge colonists gained from anthropologists' reports helped them transform African culture. How can anthropologists be trusted to tell the stories of people when they have been known to use their expertise to devastating ends, as seen in colonialism?

I learned from completing this first assignment at the university that I was academically ready for Penn. The workload was much more challenging than that at CCP, but I had the necessary foundation to adjust to it. Our class discussion and materials showed me that I was in for an intriguing learning experience, and my voice and presence in that classroom and on campus were necessary. I got the sense that the issues of Africa were largely debated and discussed by intellectuals outside of it, not Africans.

My studies almost derailed during my first semester at Penn. In the summer of 2015, shortly before I began my classes at Penn, my family and I took a vacation in my home country, Senegal, and when we returned, we brought my mother with us. She was supposed to stay with us for two months and then return to Senegal. But my mother had unstable health and was fragile to the point where she couldn't turn the doorknob to open the front door of our house. She became seriously ill a month into my first semester at the university. I took her to a clinic for blood work on a Friday and received a call from that clinic early Saturday morning telling me that I should take her to the emergency room because her phosphate levels were too high. That morning, my mom was admitted to the emergency room at the Hospital of the University of Pennsylvania, where my husband later brought me my computer and books, so I could study and write as I waited. Doctors and nurses hooked my mother up to machines from morning to night to reduce the levels of phosphate in her blood. I learned that high phosphate levels could remove calcium from the body, which weakened bones and could lead to heart attack, stroke, and even death.

That night, in the emergency room, my mom was diagnosed with polycystic kidney disease, which meant cysts had developed around her kidneys, enlarged them, and led to their loss of function over time. Since my mom didn't speak English, I was also her translator, so a doctor told me to tell her that 90 percent of her kidneys didn't function, which meant she would have to be on dialysis treatment three times a week. (Dialysis removes waste and excess fluid from the blood when the kidneys don't function properly and involves transferring one's blood to a machine to clean it.) I shared the news with her. My mom had learned years before that she had kidney problems; however, she wasn't formally diagnosed or told how damaged her kidneys were. She had told me she didn't feel well and had problems with her kidneys, but I didn't know what that really meant. Like many people in Senegal, my mom was prescribed medication after medication and asked to complete blood test after blood test, without having clarity about what was truly happening with her health. So the American doctors' diagnosis of kidney failure confirmed what she anticipated, which was why she took the news with calm.

The doctors transferred my mom to the intensive care unit, where I stayed with her overnight. I asked her night shift doctor to repeat her diagnosis to me and share more details about what her treatment would entail. As the doctor repeated that my mom's life would depend on getting dialysis three times a week, a flood of tears started running down my face. This time, I heard the doctor's message. I told the doctor that my mom and I separated when I was ten years old and that her visit to the U.S. was supposed to help us reconnect, and now we were focusing on her life-or-death situation. My tears kept flowing as I spoke. "I'm a student at Penn and just started my first semester; I have three kids; I'm married; I don't have the money for mom's treatment." The doctor said that the hospital would connect me with social workers and other support staff so that my mother could start dialysis once discharged. That day, I became my mom's caretaker.

I didn't resent my mom, but I resented the situation that I suddenly found myself in while working toward building a solid economic foundation for my family. My mom didn't want to burden me but had no other choice but to lean on me because my dad had passed and my brother wasn't yet able to support her. I had two choices: figure out how to help my mom in the U.S. or return her to Senegal knowing that, without dialysis, her days were numbered. With my husband's support, I chose to help my mom become a legal permanent resident in America while getting necessary ongoing dialysis treatment. This meant my responsibilities multiplied, my studies risked falling apart, and our home suddenly had an unexpected long-term addition to accommodate.

At the same time, I handled other transitions and demands in my life. Ibra entered school in prekindergarten, Aissata started sixth grade, and Amadou, whom I had homeschooled for the fifth and sixth grades to give him individualized attention to his academics, returned to school for seventh grade. I continued to help my children with homework and their after-school activities. Soon after graduating from CCP, I was hired for freelance reporting jobs by the *Philadelphia Tribune*, a publication covering stories about African Americans throughout Philadelphia, and the *University City Review*, which reported on West Philadelphia and Center City communities. I was also offered a volunteer position at the *Daily Pennsylvanian*, which reported on news about Penn and surrounding areas. So I really had my hands full, and fitting in my mom's three weekly dialysis sessions as well as her overall integration into American society was far from easy.

I continued to adjust and deal with the many changes and challenges in my day-to-day life. My days started at 5:30 a.m. I got myself ready for the day and the children for school and dropped them off there. I visited my mom at the hospital and went to school. Throughout the day, I spoke on the phone with my mom's doctors, nurses, and social workers, receiving up to twenty calls per day, and checked in with my husband by phone at different times as well. I conducted interviews for my newspaper assignments. After my classes, I returned to visit my mom at the hospital, then went back home and helped the kids with homework. My husband and I took turns taking the kids to their after-school activities. I fixed dinner and we ate, and Amadou and Aissata took turns washing dishes. I read bedtime stories to the kids, and they went to bed at around 8:00 p.m. Then I chatted with my husband about the events of the day and made plans for the following one. I studied for my classes and drafted my newspaper articles. I went to bed anywhere from 10:30 p.m. to midnight or 1:00 a.m. on extra-busy days. I restarted that routine the next day.

At times, I worried that I would lose my mind from the number of responsibilities tied to mom's health, all heaped on me simultaneously:

- establishing her dialysis treatment three times a week, with the transportation and diet connected to it
- constantly speaking on her behalf and translating for her
- starting her immigration process, so she could legally remain in America for an indefinite time
- figuring out her long-term living situation in our home and how to meet the expenses

I aimed to balance my responsibilities to my marriage, my children, my studies, my reporting assignments, and my mother's needs. Most times, I was too engulfed in the process to think about it. Only years later would I start reflecting on the hardships and lessons of that period in my life.

Quitting my studies wasn't an option for me, because I understood that my family's financial stability in the future depended on my perseverance with my education. So I kept studying, at the hospital, at Penn's libraries and outdoors on campus, at our home, during my kids' after-school activities, or while at the playground. I couldn't neglect my marriage. My husband and I had worked too hard to establish a foundation for our family, so I kept the lines of communication between us consistently open to resolve issues as they came up, such as scheduling conflicts when he took over tasks that I usually handled, like taking the kids to their after-school activities and doctors' appointments. Deprioritizing my kids wasn't an option for me, either. My kids were the reason I kept going, no matter what, so it was essential that their schooling and other routines remained on track. Reporting contributed to my sanity during that period, as it provided rare moments when I completely forgot about my own problems and responsibilities and immersed myself in issues that impacted individuals, communities, and society as a whole.

Once again, I learned that I was equipped for the challenges life presented to me, even the ones that seemed to destabilize every part of it. God manifested his presence and guidance daily, sustaining me through worries, tears, and the overwhelming weight of demands. Life could bruise me but not break me.

One example of how I dealt with my studies and my mom's hospitalization was the midterm exam in my class Introduction to Africa. Days before the exam, I told my professor that my mom was hospitalized and in critical condition and that I was her caretaker, which made it difficult for me to study for the upcoming test. My professor said that I could take the exam up to two weeks later, if necessary. I thanked the professor for her flexibility and thought about the exam extension offer but quickly concluded that my mom's situation would be ongoing for an unknown period and that I needed to take that test with all the students, as scheduled. I carried my class materials everywhere with me and studied during bus rides to and from Penn, at the hospital while visiting my mom, and at my children's after-school activities. I stayed up later and woke up earlier, all to prepare for the midterm exam, which was worth 30 percent of my overall grade in the course, and I ended up scoring 89 out of 100. That course had a total of eight tests, counting quizzes, a midterm, and a final exam. I continued to take all the tests on time and to study within the flow of my life's activities. My mindset was that I didn't have even ten minutes to waste, so I squeezed in studying every chance possible. Every night, I wrote my to-do list for the following day to remind myself of all the key activities that I needed to take care of, and throughout the day, I would check the list to stay on track. That first semester, I completed both of my courses with As, even earning an A-plus in my course Youth and Democracy in Africa!

Most importantly, I finished my first semester at Penn with an overwhelming realization of just how much the stories and histories of the African continent have been told by colonizers, not Africans. That realization led me to question everything I read about Africa and its populations and to wrestle with the profound damage of colonization and its continued negative impact on the continent. Many patterns stood out to me as I consumed the content of those courses: the violence and social, economic, political, and cultural destabilization that Africans experienced at the hands of colonizers, no matter which part of the continent I read about. There was a focus on Africans as needy and inferior and their societies as dysfunctional, as well as stories that presented Africans as foreign and uncivilized vis-à-vis Westerners and made them seem exotic. Consistently, I heard only the voices of Westerners narrating the stories and histories of Africans, and the voices of Africans, telling their own stories and histories, were missing. Everywhere, I saw the insistence on imposing Western points of view, ways of life, and values upon African populations and societies.

I agreed with one of my readings, titled "Time on the Move," by Cameroonian historian Achille Mbembe, where he argues that Africa and Africans have come to be viewed solely through a negative lens and that Westerners insist on portraying Africans as subhuman and refuse to accept them as equals because doing so would threaten the West's image of superiority in the world and dismantle the justification for its wrongdoings vis-à-vis other races. Mbembe asserts that Western political scientists, anthropologists, and historians have studied African countries from the perspective of what they are missing, what their societies "are not," rather than "what they actually are." I came away from those courses as an improved critical thinker about the world around me and beyond.

In the summer of 2017, what I learned about the history of European exploitation of Africans deeply distressed me. Our class watched one film, in particular, that drove home the evils of colonial rule in Africa. I remember feeling sick one afternoon after watching *Camp de Thiaroye* because the film depicted how French colonizers massacred African soldiers who had fought on behalf of France. *Camp de Thiaroye* offered a vivid historical insight into colonial Africa—that is, the relationship between the colonizers and the colonized. Set in 1944 in Dakar, Senegal (a French colony at the time), it told the story of some African soldiers called Senegalese *tirailleurs*, who were initially recruited from Senegal and soon from throughout Africa and who fought for the French army. These soldiers were temporarily kept in the camp at Thiaroye under the strict watchful eyes of their French commanders, who had refused to pay them their promised salaries after they returned from combat in France during World War II (1939–1945). French colonizers achieved their goal of controlling Africans through terror but failed to convince them that France's oppressive colonial rule was a "normal" way of life.

French colonizers regarded Africans' freedom of movement as a threat to their rule in West Africa. The lives of African soldiers in *Camp de Thiaroye* were tightly restricted by French officers, while a barbed wire fence surrounded the camp. The only African soldier depicted going in and out of the camp was Sergeant Diatta, who was well-educated and married to a French woman. In Dakar at large, Africans did not have access to many places, only Westerners did. Sergeant Diatta, for instance, was thrown out of a brothel after someone learned that he was an African, not a Black American. The colonizers strongly believed in segregating Africans from French citizens in order to provide the latter with better living conditions while Africans struggled for bare survival.

In *Camp de Thiaroye*, when African soldiers held their French general hostage to demand fair pay, the general finally promised them the compensation they had earned. However, later, in the middle of the night, this general sent tanks to massacre those African soldiers; most of them died as the camp was reduced to rubble. The film showed that violence and terror could not be long-term strategies for governing people. Sooner or later, oppressed people will demand humane living conditions through riots, violence, and ongoing revolts.

I came to the conclusion that international relations was a Eurocentric field of study. I studied the history of U.S. diplomacy since 1776, and every time the professor mentioned African Americans, it was in the context of slavery or other forms of oppression they suffered, not for their contributions, until 1977, when President Carter appointed African American civil rights leader Andrew Young to serve as the U.S. ambassador to the United Nations. One day after class, I asked the professor about the contributions of African Americans to U.S. diplomacy, to which he responded he wasn't an expert in African American history. My question was about American history, which is intertwined with African American history, but the professor viewed the two as separate histories. That reminded me of the importance of having diverse professors in the classroom, not just for their knowledge on any given subject but also for how they contextualize that knowledge to what and how they teach. My enduring question was, Why were Black people so blatantly ignored and excluded as thinkers, leaders, contributors, and protagonists in both African and American history?

As an English minor, I took courses exploring literature, concentrating on the African diaspora. For example, in the summer of 2017, I took a class focused on Black women writers. I read and examined stories by African American women authors, such as *Their Eyes Were Watching God* by Zora Neale Hurston, *The Bluest Eye* by Toni Morrison, *The Women of Brewster Place* by Gloria Naylor, *Gather Together in My Name* by Maya Angelou, and *Sara's Psalms* by Florence Ladd. These stories revealed themes of pain, discovery, and overcoming continual adversity, the good and evil in human beings, the courage to find one's own path, the sacrifices of Black women and society's rejection of them as human beings, including their hair, skin color, and body size.

As I read about the experiences of Black women in the United States from slavery to the present day, my takeaway was that their story has been that of abuse and pain but also that of resilience and progress. Black women found the courage to resist and persist in the face of overwhelming oppression and stress, from the enslaved woman to the First Lady of the United States. These women did not sit back and accept the status quo; they were visionaries, educators, community organizers, storytellers, activists, pioneers, diplomats, historians… With each successive generation, these women have chipped away the oppressive walls that have encircled their destiny. The key ingredient that has propelled Black people forward, including Black women, has been resilience.

I also learned about poetry, in a course titled Writing Toward Diaspora in the summer of 2018. In analyzing poems, I appreciated the flexibility and creativity through which one can convey thoughts in this genre of writing, especially the ability to express a complex message in a brief but layered manner. Below is one poem I wrote in that class, titled "Meanwhile, We Survive…"

> *Before Him, thousands of years before Him, Egypt*
>   *was here with its math, its science, its medicine,*
>   *its technology, its arts, its people…*
> *Before Him, hundreds of years before Him, the kingdom*
>   *of Ghana was here with its gold, its army, its people…*
> *Before Him, hundreds of years before Him, the*
>   *kingdom of Benin was here with its*
>   *bronze, its ivory, its copper, its people…*
> *Before Him, hundreds of years before Him, the*
>   *kingdom of Mali was here with its vast*
>   *land, its cowry shell currency, its people…*
> *Meanwhile He imagined Us, depicted*
>   *Us as animalistic creatures*
> *Then He "discovered" Us, wrote about Us as "savage" beings*
> *He chopped up His African pie in the Berlin Conference*
> *We no longer recognize Ourselves*
> *Our ancestors chained and sandwiched in Gorée Island*
> *Tossed in the Atlantic Ocean*

Hanged in North American trees
Massacred in villages
Massacred in Soweto
Massacred in Arkansas
Nkrumah is president!
Mandela is president!
Obama is president!
Kingdom, slavery, colonialism, apartheid,
    "independence," racism
Macron still tells Us what language to
    speak, what currency to use
Our ancestors, our youth are still drowning
    in the Atlantic Ocean
Amadou Diallo.
Michael Brown.
Eric Garner.
Trayvon Martin.
They. still. can't. Breathe.
Soweto still burns, still rises
Mandela promised freedom
Winnie dies waiting for freedom
Obama promised hope
John Lewis lives waiting to exhale
Meanwhile Trevor Noah makes Us laugh...

My intellectual experience at Penn—reading, examining, discussing, and writing about a wide range of topics—allowed me to broaden my perspective not only about what I was learning but also about myself and my place in the world.

I became even more focused on studying global affairs at Penn as an inaugural Perry World House student fellow during the

2016–2017 academic year. Our cohort, consisting of twenty-five Penn undergraduates, was the first ever selected for this fellowship. I attended weekly seminars led by thinkers and policy practitioners across fields and regions; got front-row seats to listen to distinguished leaders of the U.S. and other countries around the world; produced a yearlong group policy project on increasing women's political participation in democratic countries; and went on visits, including to the U.S. Department of State, the U.S. Department of Defense, and the Brookings Institution in Washington, DC.

Some experiences that stayed with me included listening to former Vice President Joe Biden engage in three different dialogues on the Penn campus. During his dialogue with former Mexican president Felipe Calderón on September 26, 2017, Biden said that immigrants have made America great, and the U.S. has been able to attract the best people of every culture in the world, those with the most optimism, courage, and strength. That day, after the dialogue, I met Biden at a Perry World House reception. He was surrounded by many people as I approached him. I shook hands with him, and we chatted. I felt like I already knew Biden both because of his friendly demeanor and because I had watched him many times in the news, so I launched into a conversation.

"Vice President Biden, I just left from listening to your talk," I said. "I especially liked the part when you talked about how immigrants have been a part of what makes America great."

"That's a fact," Biden confirmed.

"I really appreciate your words," I responded.

"Tell me about you!" Biden inquired.

"My name is Aminata Sy," I started. "I'm an inaugural Perry World House student fellow; I researched with them last year. I study international relations with an English minor at Penn; I'm originally from Senegal and came to the U.S. in 2001."

"We are happy to have you here. Do great things, kiddo!" Biden exclaimed.

"Thank you! I will!" I responded.

Two other people interrupted to talk to Biden and take pictures, but I waited. And when they left, I told Biden, "I didn't take a picture yet. I want to remember this," and he replied, "Of course."

I asked a young man standing near us to take a picture of Biden and me and thanked him for capturing the moment. Biden wore a navy-blue suit with an American flag pinned on the upper left lapel, a white dress shirt, and a tie with red and dark blue stripes. He held a glass of what seemed like apple juice in his right hand as I stood near him, both of us smiling at the camera. Biden behaved like an average guy, interacting with many different people while attempting to give each person focused attention. I left the event thinking about how humble and approachable he appeared and how Penn provided a space for its students to engage with some of the most influential individuals in the country and the world while making it seem just like another day on campus.

I had a similar feeling about the level of access Penn provided to its students when I met President Elbegdorj of Mongolia at a reception on campus after his lecture there in September 2016. I had attended the lecture and was one of the students who asked him a question. President Elbegdorj had said he cherished Mongolian culture, so I asked him to tell us more about it. Afterward, President Elbegdorj headed to a reception packed with students, many of us chatting with him and taking photos. As I rode home on the bus that Friday evening, I thought, What would the West Philadelphia I lived in be like if every child and young person had the access and opportunities that Penn offers its students? Penn was physically located in West Philadelphia, but a world away from the poverty, violence, and lack of opportunity that people experienced in my neighborhood, just blocks from the university.

Another experience that stayed with me was participating in a seminar given by a long-time British politician in March 2017. She said that in policymaking people operate in gray areas, with limited information and choices. Therefore, good judgment was the most important attribute to develop in decision-making, and foreign policy issues often needed comprehensive solutions based on input from different stakeholders and countries. She added that legislation is a collaborative effort that takes time, which means people can accomplish much more if they're prepared not to take the credit for the end result. She also said that women in public life have a harder time and are often defined by their looks, not their substance.

The collective wisdom of leaders and students whom I engaged with, listened to, and shared spaces with led me to conclude that we were all trying to make sense of life at different levels, in our different ways, with different focuses. The perspectives of prominent leaders were important, but so was my perspective and that of each student. The problems in my neighborhood, city, country, and the world demanded individual and combined efforts for short- and long-term solutions. That's why, as my fellowship with Perry World House ended, and I was asked for my feedback on the program, I suggested attracting more Black students into the program to broaden the perspectives in research and ultimately policy prescriptions. I was the only Black woman in our cohort.

I believed then as I do today that the voices of more Black people are necessary in policy conversations because no one understands their realities more than themselves—people whose ancestors were brought to the United States against their will as well as people, like myself, who immigrated to the country from the African continent and other places around the world. We each have a unique story to tell about our own experiences as well as a collective story about what it means to be Black in America.

Policy is about people's lives, so to create policies that improve lives you have to understand people and their stories, past and present, and those individuals need to be a part of shaping those policies. I've learned that we're the sum of our life experiences and that those experiences shape our worldviews and inform our choices and decisions.

Not that my experiences at CCP and Penn were all wonderful. At each school, there were some unpleasant moments. At CCP, two of my courses, one in English and one in history, were taught by professors who didn't know how to teach. In one, an English course, the professor paced back and forth in front of the class while mumbling through his lectures and didn't provide clear guidance about how to complete the main research paper he required. So I had to lean on tutors' support to understand and execute the research assignment. In the other course, one in history, the professor sat in front of the class and read assigned materials instead of discussing and analyzing them with the students. In both courses, I couldn't wait to move on.

At Penn, in one of my English literature courses, the professor spoke too loudly through her lectures and didn't encourage open discussion. One day at the end of that course, I chatted with a classmate who was in her last year at Penn.

"How was your experience at Penn?" I asked her.

"Penn taught me a lot," the classmate responded. "But it's a very stressful and intense place; I wouldn't want to spend any more time here. For example, I liked our class but the professor was kind of mean, and I thought that was unnecessary. When I did her readings, I couldn't even write a response for a long time. I just froze."

"Her class was my least favorite at Penn so far," I responded. "I knew how to write and analyze texts before I came to her class. Her assignments were not harder than in my previous classes, but she made students feel like they didn't know what they were doing. Every time I left her class, I had a headache because of her yelling and the tense environment."

"Me too! I had headaches too," the classmate concurred. "I thought it was just me."

"No, it wasn't just you; I think we were all overwhelmed by the way she taught," I replied. "She said she encouraged open discussion, but every time a student spoke, she shut her down. When I was in her class, I thought, 'I just want to finish and get out of here.'"

"That's exactly how I feel about Penn; I just want to finish and get out of here," the classmate added.

"Good luck with everything," I said. "Hopefully, once you step out of Penn, you'll have time to reflect and find some good memories."

"I probably will, once I have time," the classmate concluded.

More than anything, that professor sowed doubt in our intellectual abilities, one of the worst things an educator can do to students.

Then, in the spring of 2018, I encountered a librarian who dismissed my question during a session meant to support our class with our senior thesis research papers in international affairs. After the librarian presented the different research resources available to Penn students, I raised my hand and asked for sources on African immigrant experiences in Philadelphia and throughout the U.S. The librarian dismissed my question as irrelevant to the session. I didn't say anything in response, but he lost me for the rest of his presentation.

After the session, I went straight to our professor, who was at the back of the room and had witnessed the exchange. I said to the professor that he knew my senior thesis topic and that the librarian's dismissiveness was unacceptable because his role was to support students, not to disregard inquiries. I asked that he talk to the librarian about the situation so that he wouldn't make the same mistake in future sessions. The professor did so, and as I was leaving the room, the librarian said to me that he didn't know that my question was relevant to my senior thesis research and apologized for his behavior, but I never reached out to him for support again. Instead, I chose to work with librarians who were open to my inquiries and pointed me in the right direction for my research. I ended up writing a well-sourced 117-page senior thesis paper titled "Culturally Responsive Teaching for Immigrant and First-Generation Children of African Background in the Diaspora" and presented my research at the Penn International Relations Program Research Conference in April 2019.

Throughout all my experiences in college, both good and bad, I chose to focus on the bigger picture of learning. I couldn't control who taught me or how they taught me, but I could always control how I responded to the instructors' teachings and their behaviors. In a way, having a poor instructor is like any other adversity: you can't change your instructor, but you can choose how you respond to the challenge.

Ultimately, my eagerness to wrap up school at Penn was less about the institution itself and my experiences there and more about the fact that I was burned out from years of studying while juggling many other responsibilities. I applied to Penn, in part, because I wanted to be among the most competitive minds in America and the world, to further push myself to improve intellectually. I wanted to discover what it meant to study at an Ivy League institution like Penn. Could I compete at that level? What were Penn students like? What were Penn professors like? What kind of resources and opportunities were available to students?

Penn lived up to my expectations in having students who were competitive both in and outside of the classroom and top professors in their fields. The pressure for a student to do more and be more was an institutional norm, so mental health problems remained pervasive. Many students studied hard, partied hard, participated in multiple extracurricular activities, and prepared for careers after Penn. I reminded myself to only pursue selective extracurricular activities, though exposed to many options, such as internship opportunities in Washington, DC, in the context of policy and international affairs.

The average Penn student came from a well-off family, American or foreign. I once shared a class with the son of a CNN talk show host. In 2016, as a reporter for the *Daily Pennsylvanian*, I covered a Penn graduation ceremony that included the daughter of a U.S. presidential candidate and the granddaughter of the sitting U.S. vice president; both men were in the audience.

The most frequent question I got from people at Penn was, "What does your husband do?" My response to that question was always the same: "My husband is a parking attendant." People didn't seem interested in talking more about my husband after hearing about his position. I married my husband not for what he did but for who I believed he was, a responsible and decent human being whom I could build a life with. By contrast, social class and titles were very important in the Penn world. More than anything, I learned at Penn that the people who studied and taught there were human beings just like me, regardless of our differences in social standing. Whatever they could achieve academically and professionally, I could.

By the time I reached my last year at Penn, I had a solid understanding of what makes an excellent teacher. Teaching well is a combination of having knowledge specific and contextual to the subject at hand and being able to articulate that information to students in an accessible way, clearly communicating expectations and how students can meet those expectations, and listening attentively to learners.

Also, effective teaching aims to meet students at their levels, adapting lessons, curriculum content, and teaching style to learners' ways of understanding materials, to their interests, and to their backgrounds, while being humble enough to learn from students and to adjust teaching accordingly. Teaching well also means creating a space where learners feel comfortable enough to contribute to class discussions and share their thoughts, providing support to students when needed, and guiding them to resources that facilitate their growth. The instructor needs to have a relaxed and confident demeanor while teaching, as this sets students at ease and makes them more receptive to the information being conveyed.

Clearly, therefore, just because someone has knowledge of a subject doesn't mean that person can teach it well. But at the same time, it's important to remember that teaching is one of the most difficult professions. Even mediocre teachers deserve respect and compensation because their work is both vital and difficult. I carry with me the memories of excellent teachers who influenced my growth and my definition of what I could achieve through learning, but I'm also grateful for teachers who were maybe less inspired but nevertheless broadened and deepened my fund of knowledge.

Sharing my educational journey with my family and celebrating my graduation milestones with them remain my proudest accomplishments from my years of schooling. Despite the focus I had to give to my academic responsibilities, I prioritized helping my children in their schooling and making sure they had fun as well and enjoyed their childhoods. My husband and I made a great team in my education journey! I kept my husband informed about my academic struggles, progress, and accomplishments and leaned on his support in juggling the claims of my education and our family. We supported my mom in surviving a deadly disease and integrating into American society. During my CCP graduation, Amadou wept tears of joy as he said, "Mommy, you did it while teaching me and taking care of us. And you graduated top of your class." I remember the bright sunshine that day, the smiles on the faces of my husband and children, the roses in the bouquet that my husband and Aissata surprised me with, and the pride of accomplishing something I didn't think possible for me. Everyone has both unique blessings and unique burdens; it's important to focus on and appreciate the blessings and not allow the burdens to overwhelm you to a point where you can't move forward.

For my Penn graduation, my family was there too. I graduated from Penn on May 20, 2019, with a bachelor's degree, cum laude with distinction, in international relations and English. Aissata took photographs of me and Ibra in our matching navy-blue caps and gowns at various sites on the campus. I held the hand of seven-year-old Ibra, who experienced every moment with me, even walking across the graduation stage and being congratulated by the dean. Amadou filmed the ceremony while my husband, mom, and daughter witnessed the event from the audience. I thanked God for giving me the strength and courage to push through daily challenges and to graduate. I reaffirmed my belief that whatever is meant for me in my lifetime I will get. Nothing is impossible if it's meant for me. Nothing is impossible for you, either.

Chapter Five

Exploring My Gifts

WHEN I WAS EIGHT YEARS OLD, I TOLD MY MOM THAT I wanted to be a journalist. In Kinshasa, I used to watch TV5, a French news broadcast, with my mom, and I admired a French journalist whose parents were from Ivory Coast, in West Africa. I appreciated her knowledge and communication skills. "I'll become a journalist just like this woman," I would say to my mom.

My unofficial storytelling journey started in 2009 when I took up journaling. I wrote about my daily activities with my children and sometimes reflected on a thought, a situation, or a book that I had read. I later realized that journaling strengthened my grasp of English, improved my writing skills, and clarified my thoughts. Below are some of my journal entries from October 2010, two years before I began my studies at CCP.

October 14, 2010

Today, the weather is beautiful; it's sunny, breezy, and a little bit cold. Amadou and Aissata didn't go to school, so at 12:00 pm we went to play tennis until 1:45 pm. Then we went to eat lunch; then we went to the library. I did some reading and writing while they played on the computers and did some games with the librarian. We left at 5:00 pm and went to the YMCA. We played until 5:15 pm, and Amadou went to his karate class, which lasted until 6:15 pm. Aissata and I went home and came back again to pick up Amadou. We got home at 6:30 pm. I cooked dinner, we ate, and the kids had free time until 8:30 pm. We did some writing and reading together. They went to bed at 9:00 pm. We really had a wonderful day!

October 17, 2010

Just me and my daughter. We walked to the park. It was really beautiful outside. The sun was very bright with a little bit of breeze—the kind of breeze that makes you feel like you could sit in the sun all day without burning your skin. We chatted along the way. When we got there, we did some counting and spelling games. Then we did some climbing and sliding. Two girls invited us to jump rope, and we did. I love to watch her express herself. There is something about the innocence of a child that I feel should never leave us. Because once it does, we start seeing the world with whole new eyes.

October 18, 2010

Over the weekend, I studied so hard for my GED classes, as if I had a big test coming my way. This is the kind of desire for learning that I feel. Now more than ever before, I feel like if I don't give up, I can move forward beyond where I am today. Now I'm always looking forward to reading a book or writing about something. I can see my progress with every additional book that I read. After so many years of not studying, I feel blessed to be able to have the desire and ability to study. I owe this to my children. Because of my willingness to help them study, I've learned so much along the way. If it wasn't for them, I would've never pushed myself this hard.

My desire to continue to improve my writing led me to CCP's student newspaper, the *Vanguard*. As a CCP student, I had been reading the *Vanguard* regularly and thought contributing to the publication would be a good way for me to continue to improve my writing. One summer afternoon in 2013, I went to the small office of the *Vanguard* and found the editor-in-chief working on his desktop computer. Hesitant and nervous, I introduced myself and told him that I was interested in writing for the *Vanguard*. He asked me if I had a writing sample to show him, and I said that I could share one of the essays I'd written for English 101. I used the other desktop computer in the office to email him an essay. He read my essay and said he had never written such a solid paper in any of his own English classes. He welcomed me to the *Vanguard* team, first as an opinion writer and later as a reporter.

At the *Vanguard*, I continued to practice the craft of writing and to develop my voice as a writer. I got into the habit of observing the scene around me more closely and constantly thinking about writing on topics useful to CCP's student body. Some topics were relevant to the day-to-day life of a student, such as time management, the value of tutoring, the importance of believing in one's abilities, the best approach to a math course, or ways to become a "master student." Other articles explored larger social issues in Philadelphia and the United States, like the intersection of privacy, individual freedom, and technology; the importance of an education; race relations; racism in the education system and its impact on Black boys; police killing of Black boys and men; gun violence; and wealth and income inequality.

I wrote for the *Vanguard* for seventeen months. In one story, titled "Philly Bloodshed Similar to That of Iraq," I explored the skyrocketing gun violence in Philadelphia that its residents had come to view as "normal" and the devastating consequences of these killings. I wrote an article titled "The Killing of Michael Brown," in which I reported on the disconnect between Black and White communities in Ferguson, Missouri, that contributed to the police killing of Michael Brown, an eighteen-year-old Black man, and the outrage of Ferguson's Black residents. In another article, titled "Race Relations in America Five Years after Obama's Election," published on February 18, 2014, I saw how my voice, prose, and thoughts had sharpened over time. Here is an excerpt:

> Today, too many Black students are still reading below their grade levels. Too many Black students are not graduating from high school. Too many Black students are not attending college. And too many young Black people are trapped in the justice system. All of these realities inevitably lead to a life of poverty and struggle, which explains the income and wealth gap between blacks and whites... America is 149 years removed from slavery, 60 years removed from the desegregation of public schools, and 49 years removed from the passing of the Voting Rights Act. All of these changes have been critical in improving race relations in America. But at the same time, the horrific history of racism has continued to negatively impact African-Americans' lives. Lawmakers cannot afford to take the issue

of racism lightly and forget its history if they truly want America to be a more fair and equal country.

The more I wrote for the *Vanguard*, the more I gained speed and clarity in the writing process and the confidence to approach just about anyone on the CCP campus, including the college president, to request an interview. An added perk was that I started to write papers for my courses in half the time it used to take me! One example was an introductory class in political science, where the professor assigned us to read a book and then summarize and respond to it based on concepts learned in class. I handed the professor my final paper for that assignment in his office before we even discussed the book in class. Through practice, my mind was being trained to analyze big problems and try to make sense of them. I was offered the position of editor-in-chief for the *Vanguard*, but I declined it because I was homeschooling Amadou at the time and preparing to transition to a university.

During my final semester at CCP, in the spring of 2015, CCP leaders selected me to be the student representative journalist on a panel with three prominent Philadelphia journalists who would question the Democratic mayoral candidates on issues impacting the city's residents. I represented both the CCP student body and the school. Before the event, I had gone around the campus to ask CCP students about issues that mattered to them most and used their answers to formulate questions for the candidates. I ended up asking two of those questions of all of the mayoral candidates—one focusing on the need for job creation and the other on giving formerly incarcerated people a second chance in society.

On the night of April 9, 2015, I stepped onto the forum stage at the CCP main campus. The bright lights were fixed on the mayoral candidates, panelists, and moderator. On one side, there was a table and chairs for the four journalists, including me, and on the other side a table and chairs for the six mayoral candidates. Our names and titles were displayed in front of us. At the center of the stage stood a podium for the moderator. I sat next to the managing editor of the *Philadelphia Tribune*. The audience sat in the dark, facing the stage, while a camera crew filmed the entire forum, which would later be televised. Surveying the scene before the mayoral debate started, I thought about how I started writing and reporting and how it led to this critical moment in my journalism journey.

My presence was a voice that represented thousands of people at CCP and across Philadelphia. I had done the homework and knew the questions I would ask, but nevertheless, I felt the weight of the moment. When my turn came to ask a question, I owned the moment by staying focused on the task, making frequent eye contact with the candidates, reading from my notes but also speaking from memory. My voice echoed with resolve. I had never been in a televised event before or participated in an event that could impact so many people once one of those candidates assumed the office of mayor.

After the forum, many people complimented me for having done a great job. I was especially pleased that my husband and children witnessed the occasion as audience members. They had watched me day after day studying for so many hours and always writing or reporting one story or another. That moment represented a culmination of an outcome worth celebrating both as a journalist and student, an accomplishment that belonged to my family just as much as it did to me. In less than two and half years, I had made so much academic and professional progress, while at the same time raising kids, honoring my commitment to my marriage, and dealing with the general pressures of life. That experience reminded me of the importance of being prepared not just for my own sake but for that of others. The work that I had put into preparing for that evening's event served the student body of the college and Philadelphians in general by highlighting issues that impacted their lives every day.

Seeing how much preparation meant to my progress, I even wrote an article for the *Vanguard,* published on November 17, 2014, and titled "Are You Ready to Be a Master Student?" In it, I shared with other CCP students what I had learned so far about succeeding in college:

- Find out how you best process information and shape your study techniques around it
- Be honest about your weaknesses and work to improve them
- Set personal standards of excellence
- Engage in extracurricular activities that align with your areas of interest
- Make contributions to your campus community and focus on improving your skills
- Manage your time effectively
- Study your instructors' teaching styles and expectations so you can position yourself to perform well in class

I wrote, "No matter how much you may be struggling in a particular subject, as long as you first acknowledge it and tirelessly work at it, you will succeed. In the end, you will be proud of yourself and gain a high level of self-confidence."

Having had a fruitful experience for CCP's student newspaper, I continued to pursue journalism after graduation. For six years, I reported or wrote for different publications in Philadelphia, including the *Philadelphia Tribune,* the *Daily Pennsylvanian, 34th Street* magazine, *University City Review,* the *Philadelphia Inquirer,* and *WHYY.* I wrote at least 150 published articles and interviewed more than 260 people.

I liked the process of coming up with a story idea, brainstorming about it, pitching it to an editor, interviewing people and doing research, drafting the article and editing it, taking photos for it, and having it published. Experiencing the process of turning an idea in my mind into a concrete story that people could touch, read, think about, and even act on was fulfilling to me. I listened to people's hopes, dreams, fears, issues, frustrations, struggles, ideas, and desires, and captured them in my notes. I talked to individuals across many walks of life to understand their perspectives. I researched past events to better understand current situations. To remain informed, I paid attention to local, national, and international events covered in the news.

What became clear to me was that people wanted to be heard, seen, understood, and included and that often those suffering the most were heard the least, and their issues were the most neglected. In writing and reporting, I learned that my voice mattered, both for what I had to say and for the many voices that spoke through mine.

Many stories that I reported on stayed with me, among them the story of Gorée Island. During my visit to Senegal in the summer of 2015, my children, some cousins, and I went to this World Heritage Site, a vibrant, colorful place that welcomes tourists from around the world. I took that opportunity to report on Gorée Island for the *Philadelphia Tribune*. That day, the beach and restaurants were packed with people. We ate at a restaurant named La Retrouvaille, or the Reunion, a family business that had been in operation for years. My children and their cousins enjoyed the island's beach—finding seashells and diving into the water—while I spoke with Goreans about the island, walked around its concrete streets, and took in the colorful buildings and the artwork displayed for sale at various locations. People chatted and laughed, and vendors called me to see their merchandise.

Goreans offered a tour or pointed me in the right direction as I strolled toward "The House of Slaves," where many Africans were once held captive. For centuries, European colonizers, including the Dutch, English, Portuguese, and French, supplied enslaved Africans to the United States, the Caribbean, and Brazil. The island had about twenty prisons for enslaved Africans, who were kidnapped from different parts of West Africa and transferred there to be shipped to the Americas, mostly to labor on plantations.

"The House of Slaves" on Gorée Island remained a chilling reminder of an atrocious past—and of how horribly human beings can treat one another for money, power, and control. When I stood inside a tiny cell in "The House of Slaves," a dark space, with thick air and no windows, after about five minutes I couldn't breathe, but European colonizers sandwiched dozens of Africans into that space for months. Those who got sick were thrown into the ocean to avoid spreading illnesses. Mothers and their children were kept in separate cells, and those who deviated from the colonizers' rules were shoved into low-ceilinged cells for further punishment.

I saw some iron shackles that European colonizers put around the necks and feet of their African captives. Many Africans died in agony in those cells. I imagined them sitting close together, their shackled arms resting on their bent knees. I imagined their moans of pain and their yearning for home. Goose bumps of horror covered my skin; my eyes watered with sympathy. I wondered, *How can human beings inflict such pain on other human beings?*

The space reminded me of both the evil and the resilience in human beings. I wondered how anyone survived imprisonment on Gorée Island or the enslavement that followed in the Americas. I stood at the "Door of No Return," the final door through which European colonizers dragged enslaved Africans to load them onto boats bound for the Americas, never again to see their homeland. I thought about the many roots cut off, the humanity and cultural richness stripped away, the human history disrupted, and the many lives lost. Many people died chained in those boats, and their oppressors tossed them into the Atlantic Ocean. Others threw themselves into the water; they preferred death to enslavement.

The Statue of the Liberation from Slavery on the island also captured my attention. This statue depicted an African woman and man standing on a wide-top drum. The topless African woman faces the man, her arms encircling his waist. The shirtless African man holds his hands up, broken chains dangling from his wrists, his eyes turned toward the sky. This statue symbolized freedom while showing the scars of slavery. Gorée Island itself felt like a combination of pain and joy and a concrete reminder that we can't take freedom for granted, that human beings are capable of building and destroying lives and societies on a massive scale, and that we must remain vigilant to avoid repeating the evils of our past, to live in a better present, and to safeguard a more just future for generations to come.

I reported on present-day racism too and its impact on Black populations in America, both native-born and immigrant—racism that cut across contexts and systems and affected education, employment, housing, quality of life, and encounters with law enforcement. One example was a story I reported for *34th Street* magazine, on an incident where six Black freshmen at Penn were added to a GroupMe chat that displayed photos of lynching.

I also reported on educational disparities in Philadelphia. One example was a story I covered for the *Daily Pennsylvanian* on local learners from three different high schools and their struggles to get admitted to Penn, a university in their own neighborhood. Students from two of the high schools had little to no hope of getting into Penn; they were Black Americans from low-income families, and many of them were immigrants. In fact, for the majority of the students I interviewed from these two schools, Penn seemed like a distant dream. Obstacles ranged from Penn's high standards for Scholastic Aptitude Test (SAT) scores, fear of rejection, and the university's fast-paced environment to lack of interaction with the institution's admission representatives, English language barriers, and insufficient financial aid. Academic counselors expressed frustration over Penn's neglect of their students and disregard for their schools. In the one high school whose students had a chance of being accepted at Penn, learners stretched themselves thin by taking many advanced placement classes while engaging in different extracurricular activities to strengthen their college applications.

What stayed with me the most remained the students' passion and determination to improve their lives and those of their families and contribute to society through their future studies at universities and their eventual careers. The question was, which institution would have the good fortune to open its doors to young people ready to do their part?

I also reported a story for the *University City Review* on the desire of African immigrant and first-generation American youth in West Philadelphia to stay in touch with their cultures through learning Pulaar, a language spoken in several West African countries, including Senegal and Mauritania, and to have a cultural center that better connected them as a community. Among the fifteen children I interviewed was a seventeen-year-old from Senegal who told me that culture was the anchor of his life and that's why he believed it was so important.

As I listened to the children one by one, I thought about the price of immigrating to another country, which I knew all too well. Families who come to the United States from French-speaking countries in Africa must restart their lives, learn English, and familiarize themselves with American culture, society, and institutional systems, such as education, healthcare, and labor. Some immigrant parents will never integrate into American society because their priority is survival—feeding their families, putting a roof over their heads, and attempting to keep up with the bills that seem to come every day. Numerous immigrant parents and their children end up experiencing endless difficulties because America has a fast-paced culture, where people can only dedicate a limited amount of time to support you in any area. You either integrate or you're left behind to live on the margins of society, attempting just to survive.

African immigrant children are reminded often by their peers at school that they don't belong in America and should "go back to Africa," even if they are first-generation Americans. When immigrant parents and children visit their home countries in Africa, they're welcomed by family, but soon after their arrival are asked, "When are you returning to America?" Culture reminds immigrants of who they are and where they come from, and it guides them on how to move through their different worlds. Having a sense of belonging becomes a perpetual battle because immigrants become strangers in their home countries and never cease to be foreigners in their adopted country. This is what I tried to convey in the articles I wrote about the African immigrant community in West Philadelphia. Every individual's story teaches us about ourselves and our society, its limitations, injustices, and opportunities. Every individual's story tells us of someone's experience within that society and how that person contributes to our shared life. Every individual story teaches us about what it means to be a human being, our flaws, capabilities, hopes, and dreams, and how interconnected we are. Regardless of our differences, we're all people.

Chapter Six

Shaping Young Minds

"THIS IS A LABOR OF LOVE." THAT'S HOW SOME PEOPLE described the African Community Learning Program (ACLP), the nonprofit organization I founded in June 2017 with the support of my husband. I was still studying at Penn when I opened ACLP's door to students in October 2017, and I ran the program until April 2021. ACLP was an after-school program with the mission to educate, connect, empower, and support people of African background in West Philadelphia, namely, immigrants and first-generation Americans with African parents.

One reason I decided to start an after-school program supporting these students is because I'm one of them. Like these students, I've lived in between cultures and understand their struggle to integrate into American society and develop a sense of belonging. I believed that ACLP could support African diaspora students in their education, allow them to clearly see the value of their cultural heritage, and demonstrate that they, like me, could overcome significant barriers and achieve remarkable goals in their lives. I came to realize that my multicultural experiences, moving from Kinshasa to Dakar to Philadelphia and speaking multiple languages (Pulaar, Wolof, French, and later, English and some Spanish) have enriched my perspective on everything. Whether in a classroom, on assignment for a newspaper, or in my day-to-day experiences, my multicultural background has been a blessing. I believe that when African diaspora students fully embrace their cultural identity, they can become leaders who shape their families, their communities, and the world.

My husband and I started running ACLP in the basement of our home in West Philadelphia. Later we moved the after-school program to the Blackwell Library and then to Paul Robeson High School, both located in West Philadelphia. At first, we enrolled only children in the first through eighth grades but later also welcomed African diaspora high-schoolers. ACLP taught a tailored, culturally responsive, African-centered curriculum that promoted cultural pride and celebrated African heritage while helping students with homework and English literacy skills, facilitating their integration into American society through mentorship, lessons, books, educational videos, projects, trips, guest speakers, and events, all for free and all aimed at hammering home one message to the learners: you matter, and what you bring to the table matters.

As part of the curriculum, ACLP launched #500EmpoweringAfricanStories, a library of stories written and published by our volunteers and me, focusing on African diaspora individuals whom we thought our students should know about. ACLP served students with ties to eight countries: Senegal, Nigeria, Mali, Niger, Sudan, Burkina Faso, Mauritania, and Liberia.

The program expanded the students' sense of their academic possibilities, future careers, and contributions to society.

I taught ACLP learners with the help of undergraduate volunteers from Penn and Temple. We discussed various topics with the children, including languages and influential people in our own lives and in society. A participant I'll call Nabou exemplified how ACLP supported students. Nabou, an eighth-grader from Senegal who attended a public school in Philadelphia, had immigrated to the United States in September 2017 to join her parents, and her mother brought her to ACLP in February 2018. Nabou cried after school most days because she was frustrated that she couldn't understand her teachers and hurt that her peers teased her for not speaking English and for having an accent when she tried to express herself in that language.

However, just a month after she joined ACLP, in March 2018, Nabou wrote in English a story about how important her grandmother, who raised her in Senegal, was to her and read it aloud in front of students. Her presentation brought tears to my eyes because I had witnessed her growth day by day and now saw what Nabou, and every student who walked through ACLP's door, was capable of, which I already believed before I ever taught any of them. I knew that day was a turning point in Nabou's education in her new country and her integration into American society.

I taught Nabou by reading aloud to her from prekindergarten- and kindergarten-level books, pointing at words and sounding them out, moving at a slow pace, translating sentences from English to Pulaar and at times from English to French to Pulaar, stopping to make sure she understood the materials, reminding her that she would come to understand as long as she continued to practice. For instance, I read her the *Bob Books*, by Bobby Lynn Maslen, a children's book series with a simple sentence structure that helped with phonics, vocabulary, and reading comprehension. Those books had many sight words such as *he*, *had*, *has*, and *went* (words learned as a whole unit rather than phonetically) and allowed Nabou to build a foundation for her English vocabulary.

I also read Nabou books telling stories of Africans; one of them was titled *My Name Is Sangoel*, by Karen Williams and Khadra Mohammed. Sangoel, a boy from Sudan in North Africa, immigrated to the United States as a refugee. His classmates and teacher couldn't correctly pronounce his name, and that made him sad. One day, Sangoel had the idea of drawing, on a white T-shirt, pictures of a sun and a soccer ball entering a goal net and wearing it to school to teach his classmates and teacher how to say his name, and his strategy succeeded.

Nabou could see herself in stories like *My Name Is Sangoel*, which facilitated her understanding of English, captured her attention, and kept her wanting to read more and more books. I also paired Nabou with volunteers who spoke French to help with her homework, ACLP lessons, assignments, and projects. I stopped often while teaching ACLP lessons to translate what I was saying in English into Pulaar, so Nabou and other students who spoke that language could understand.

ACLP was a space where Nabou and each student could speak English with accents and mistakes and were encouraged to continue to practice and improve. Students could speak in their native languages too—Pulaar, Arabic, Mandingo, Yeruba, among others—and know that their tongues were both welcomed and celebrated. English was one language among many languages in the world; they needed to learn it to integrate into American society, but English wasn't more important than any of the other languages they spoke.

This inclusiveness allowed Nabou and her ACLP peers to learn and grow in their education and in their integration into the United States. ACLP's chant, which I wrote for our students and which we recited in many of our sessions, also reinforced the message that they mattered: "I am Africa; Africa is me. I am the world; the world is me. I have the intelligence, the courage, and the power to change the world."

A thank-you letter that an eighth grader from Nigeria wrote to me and ACLP volunteers and handed me on the last day of our first semester captured learners' experiences. This student was soft-spoken, very shy and kind, and had experienced bullying at school for having dark brown skin and for being from Africa. She ended up thriving in the after-school program. Here is what she wrote.

> Thank you for letting me be part of African Community Learning Program. I am grateful for being a part of the program. Before I joined the program, I used to think that a team is when a group of people work together. But after joining the program, I found out that a team is not just about working together but about loving, caring, motivating, encouraging, supporting, advising, collaborating, connecting, communicating, and learning each other'[s] background[s]. I appreciate you guys for making me become more bold and brave. I enjoyed working with you guys and learning each other'[s] cultures, traditions, tribes, languages, and countries. I hope to be a part of the program in the future.

ACLP students also learned a range of subjects from guest speakers. One Penn professor taught students about the history of the N'Ko language, spoken in countries such as Guinea, Mali, Ivory Coast, and Burkina Faso. A Philadelphia councilwoman told students that the histories of Africans and African Americans were connected and noted that America was open to individuals from all over the world and gave them the freedom to have their own cultures.

A lawyer and Philadelphia's first city solicitor from Africa talked to ACLP students about his journey integrating into American society as an eight-year-old boy from Zaire and discussed how he faced obstacles such as bullying, rejection, isolation, and financial hardship, and ultimately overcame them to graduate from Harvard University. One fifth grader's reaction was "I met a lawyer!" while a ninth grader concluded that "people like me can go very far in this country."

A Nigerian artist explained how he pursued his passion for art from a young age, taught himself to draw and paint, used his art to pay for his education, and later turned it into a successful career. He advised students, "Don't compare yourself to others. Be passionate, be proud of your rich cultural heritage, and dare to do great things."

The superintendent of the School District of Philadelphia visited ACLP and heard from students and their parents about their concerns. A ninth grader said, "When I was trying to speak English, people laughed at me," and a fifth grader shared, "People mess with me because I am African. But I told them I am proud to be African." I told the superintendent that whenever you're in a learning environment and you don't see yourself and people who look like you in the curriculum, that tells you that you don't matter.

ACLP hosted an event where more than seventy community members, including ACLP students and their parents, heard for the first time from Philadelphia's director of immigrant affairs, who explained her role and shared some resources available to members of the African community. Attendees voiced their concerns, including about their children's education, and expressed the need for a community center for immigrant families from Senegal and Mauritania. The different guest speakers allowed ACLP students to learn about the importance of persistence in achieving their goals and dreams, even in the face of adversities, and the value of their cultural heritage and advocating for themselves and their community.

ACLP students also learned and expanded their imaginations through trips. At the Blackwell Library in West Philadelphia, students researched and worked on group projects about African countries of their choice and on themes we had covered in class, using trifolds or PowerPoint presentations to display information and images. Then they presented their projects to the class and during the organization's annual Africa celebrations, where learners, parents, partners, and community members gathered to enjoy African foods, accept awards, and cheer on the labor of ACLP participants. Students also toured the Philadelphia NBC10 news station, where they got a behind-the-scenes look at how news is broadcast on television. An NBC10 reporter, whose parents immigrated to America from Sierra Leone, West Africa, told the students, "It doesn't matter if you were born here, if you were not born here; if you have an accent, if you don't have an accent. Hard work certainly pays off. Don't try to get rid of your culture—it's beautiful, it's necessary, it sets you apart."

At Penn, ACLP students toured the Van Pelt Library and attended a presentation about ancient manuscripts from the African continent that have survived for centuries. Students also visited Penn's Perelman School of Medicine, where African diaspora medical students described their career paths. One medical student advised ACLP learners, "Surround yourself with people who are supportive of you to help you be the best version of yourself."

At Philadelphia's City Hall, a councilwoman gave our group a private tour, and ACLP students marveled at the place, the largest municipal building in the United States. After the tour, students sat down for a chat in the office of the mayor, who said he supported a curriculum that met the cultural needs of children and their parents. These trips exposed ACLP students to educational and professional options and to places of power and influence while allowing them to see that those spaces belonged to them too.

The global COVID-19 pandemic, which changed how people around the world lived their lives, affected how ACLP operated too. ACLP's 2020–2021 school year theme was "Preparing for the Future Through Education, Excellence, and Justice." We held events and activities from May 2020 to April 2021, but in a new format. The organization went from being fully in-person to fully virtual due to the pandemic, expanded and restructured its team by creating additional task-specific positions to execute our work more efficiently, and recruited more undergraduate volunteers from Penn and graduate students from American University.

A major shift in our programming was a new focus on high school students and on a college-preparatory curriculum. Also, for the first time, ACLP's advocacy included policy work, a result of my studies at American University for a master's degree in public policy. In collaboration with ACLP volunteers, I produced three policy documents for Philadelphia policymakers and leaders in the School District of Philadelphia. These studies provided recommendations on culturally responsive teaching, in particular for immigrant students and English learners.

Advocacy was a central part of my work as ACLP's president. On a cold Tuesday night in March 2018, at the CBS News headquarters in Philadelphia, I got a chance to raise an issue of urgent importance to ACLP. The mayor was present, addressing a meeting of the Philadelphia Association of Black Journalists (PABJ), an organization that had supported my growth as a journalist. On that occasion, I asked the mayor a question about ACLP after I introduced myself as its founder and a PABJ member. "We help students of African background in West Philadelphia from first through eighth grade with homework and teach them English and an African-centered curriculum. You mentioned that education is a priority in your administration. We currently run our program in our home's basement. My question to you is, does the city have any housing opportunities for organizations like ours?" The mayor replied, "I think teaching kids about their cultural heritage is very important, especially for kids who came here at a young age and those who were born in this country trying to learn more about themselves. Our schools don't teach much of it; what I can do is take your contact information and put you in touch with [the city's chief education officer]. He may find you a classroom in a school close to where most of these students live or may suggest other partnerships." I nodded in agreement and thanked him.

Afterward, I handed the mayor ACLP's flyer and a copy of a letter our secretary had written to him about the organization. "This letter was already sent to you, but I'm hand-delivering it again," I said to the mayor. He wrapped the letter inside of the ACLP flyer and put it in his jacket. A few PABJ members told me that I had asked my question well. I got into the frequent practice of addressing questions to powerful decision-makers in our city. I had come far in my ability to speak English and could now express myself confidently in public.

Another way I advocated for ACLP students was through the media. The academic struggles and progress of African diaspora students were not part of the discourse of K–12 education in America. It was as if they were invisible children. Part of ACLP's work was to make African diaspora children visible, especially to those responsible for their education in Philadelphia. Chalkbeat Philadelphia, a nonprofit news organization covering education, interviewed me about ACLP and published an article titled "Teacher Bridges Global Divide for Philadelphia Students with African-Centered Curriculum." This story was republished by Chalkbeat's affiliated bureaus in Chicago, Detroit, Newark, New York City, and elsewhere. In the interview, my message was simple: ACLP supported students and their parents through listening to them and understanding their needs and strengths. Thousands of people around America learned about African diaspora students through that article, on the online front page of Chalkbeat Philadelphia on February 17 and 18, 2021.

Through ACLP's work, I also mentored Penn students who were interested in learning about my career path focusing on my work in education, advocacy, and social entrepreneurship. At Penn's Perelman School of Medicine, in February 2018, I gave a talk to Penn medical students, who wanted to learn through my experiences how they could impact the Philadelphia community in their future careers as physicians. I told them to consider the following questions in order to make an impact. What do you uniquely bring to the table that no one else does? Do you know your central mission well enough to pitch it to a variety of audiences? Do you listen to the people you want to serve in order to learn as much as possible about them? Are you patient?

I spoke to Wharton School students in September 2018 about some crucial skills for entrepreneurship: reaching out to people and communicating well with them, seeking support from the university community and beyond, clarifying the focus of your initiative, educating yourself continually, bracing for the long hours of work, and reflecting often on your initiative in order to improve your effectiveness.

I promoted ACLP's work, and education in general, through community engagements. In a speech titled "Celebrating Our Youth," delivered at a women's conference at Philadelphia's City Hall in March 2019, I talked about how important my education had been to me and encouraged young people to stick with theirs. Below is an excerpt from that speech.

So, for the young people here today and the not-so-young people, it's never too late to start learning. Now, this doesn't mean that education will come easy, because it won't. There will be many long days of studying, long nights of staying up to finish those essays, less and less time to spend with family and friends, less and less time to watch your favorite shows. There will even be times when you ask yourself, "Why am I sacrificing so much to get an education?" "Is education worth it?" For me, the answer to that last question is yes. Education is worth sacrificing for... I've learned that when we give up on education, we partly give up on our communities. Education is a tool that can help us achieve bigger goals that could touch many lives, close to us and far away.

A memorable community engagement was the night *Fun Times* magazine, a publication celebrating Africa and its diaspora, honored me among its Women of Influence awardees in March 2019. As drums played in the background and the audience clapped, the presenter called upon me first to receive the award and then to say a few words. I stood near the podium holding the award, behind me a collage of cover images from *Fun Times*. I stepped to the podium and started speaking by introducing myself and praising Yaye for her contributions to my life. "I was raised by a woman who had no titles, no degrees, very little financial means, but she was a very influential woman in my life and the lives of many, many others...I dedicate this award tonight to Yaye for *everything* she poured into me. Her legacy lives on in me and many lives she touched." I loved that I had the chance to publicly thank and honor Yaye, a woman who sacrificed so much and who never received an award in her lifetime.

"I thank my children who are here tonight," I continued, "—Amadou; Aissata; and Ibra, my seven-year-old, who is home—for motivating me every single day to keep going." I rejoiced that my son and daughter attended that event to experience it for themselves and that I affirmed their contribution to my life; without them, I would've never given that speech.

I went on, "I thank my husband who is also here; his name is Abdoul. My husband supports me on every level, especially with my education." The applause of the audience was interrupted by the banging drums, and my husband stood up smiling, waving at the crowd. I pointed toward him saying, "Yes, he's over there. My husband has been there with me and for me as a non-English speaker"—my voice trembled as my eyes watered—"from a GED level now to almost a BA level. I'm about to graduate from the University of Pennsylvania." The audience interjected with thunderous claps, blending with the beating drums. "And then soon to move on to a master's degree program at American University, to study public policy." More claps and drums erupted. "My husband has been there with me *every step of the way*, so I'm grateful to him." I was filled with gratitude that I had this opportunity to recognize my husband by articulating to him and everyone present just how much his support has meant to me. I ended the speech by thanking ACLP students, parents, volunteers, partners, and supporters for their participation. "All of the work that we do is community-based; we cannot do it by ourselves." I've always carried with me the memory of that night because that award was about the people who helped shape the person I've become.

Our volunteers learned as much from ACLP as our students. They gained many skills in teaching multicultural children, communication, community engagement, advocacy, leadership, management, entrepreneurship, and writing. Together, we created memories for a lifetime. One particular note from a volunteer stayed with me. "There are people who come into our lives for a season, there are those who come to stay, and yet there are those whose presence cannot be measured by time. You are the third kind. Thanks for being you."

Our volunteers and I supported non-English-speaking children in reading, writing, comprehending, and conversing in English. We witnessed shy students become confident and outspoken about their stories and cultures. We assisted struggling learners to excel in their schools and expand their views of their possibilities. I and the other ACLP staff members, as well as Africans featured in the curriculum materials, served as the mirrors of what the children could achieve in America and beyond in terms of college education, careers, and societal contribution and integration. It was an honor for me to serve my communities and country alongside my husband and the selfless and generous individuals who believed in ACLP's mission.

To be part of the African diaspora, to be Black in a largely White environment, is to constantly receive messages from the world that something is wrong about your very humanity and existence, that you're not good enough, not intelligent enough, not beautiful enough, not a contributor. I've learned that these negative messages are lies. To be part of the African diaspora, to be Black, is to have all the flaws and brilliance that exist in every human being on earth, to be enough as you are, to achieve at any level you want, to be beautiful as you are, to contribute to whoever and whatever you want.

For me, being a part of the African diaspora has meant finding ways to create connections among different groups. The collective history of the African diaspora has had the effect of separating and dividing us to a point where we don't recognize one another as being from the same continent. A big challenge that faces us, the African diaspora, is to relearn about ourselves, reconnect among ourselves, rewrite our history, and embrace our similarities and differences. Unity would allow us to address many problems and recognize our influence in our communities and the world.

An important part of knowing your value is learning about yourself and your community. Leaders are not born ready to lead; they learn over time. Ask your parents and family members questions about your roots; read the stories of people who came before you; visit places in your community that teach about history, such as museums; watch historical movies and documentaries that interest you; learn from knowledgeable people, including elders in your family.

Learning about yourself allows you to interact with the world with confidence and to make big decisions about your life—for example, deciding what university to attend, what field of study to focus on, what initiatives to undertake, whom to associate with, or what career to pursue. We have countless problems that need to be addressed, such as poverty, racism, mass incarceration, and unequal access to quality education and healthcare. We need to question why and how problems came to be, hold people in power accountable for those problems, and even offer solutions. In this entire world, there is only one of you. How will you use your uniqueness to make this world better?

As an individual, what you do matters, even in our crowded world. Social impact doesn't always involve large groups of people; sometimes it means pouring your knowledge into one person's life. In turn, that one person's growth can not only transform their own life but allow them to contribute to the lives of others. We're each capable of social impact in our own way. Each of us is unique in our particular life experiences, but we can share the things that make us who we are and make us different from everyone else; that is our offering to the world. What makes you unique and different? To whose life do you want to contribute, and why?

Chapter Seven

Learning on the Job

I BEGAN TRAINING FOR MY CAREER IN U.S. DIPLOMACY the afternoon of the day I graduated from Penn, Monday, May 20, 2019. That afternoon, I caught a train from Philadelphia to Washington, DC, to start my Rangel Program internship in the U.S. Congress. I and twenty-nine others had been selected from a nationwide pool of more than eight hundred applicants to train to become American diplomats. A U.S. Department of State program started in 2002 and administered by Howard University, the Rangel Graduate Fellowship Program aims to attract and prepare people from diverse backgrounds to work as U.S. diplomats. The 2019 Rangel Fellows cohort consisted of sixteen women and fourteen men, collectively speaking twenty-two foreign languages, with many of us having overseas experiences and family members living around the world. We were high achievers from different racial, ethnic, and geographic backgrounds and had demonstrated our ability to deal with and overcome difficult circumstances, qualities that are assets for a career in the U.S. Foreign Service.

With a majority of White and male corps since its inception in 1924, the U.S. Foreign Service has struggled with a lack of diversity and inclusion; that's why initiatives like the Rangel Graduate Fellowship Program exist. According to a January 2020 United States Government Accountability Office report titled "State Department: Additional Steps Are Needed to Identify Potential Barriers to Diversity," there were 13,260 U.S. Foreign Service Officers or diplomats, with 75 percent of them White, only 7 percent Black. Thirty-five percent were women, of which 3 percent were Black.

The PBS *American Experience* documentary *The American Diplomat* tells the story of three Black American diplomats, including Ambassador Terence Todman, dealing with systemic racial and social barriers in the United States and within the Department of State during the civil rights movement. Their pioneering accomplishments and their advocacy for a more fair and inclusive Foreign Service paved the way for future diplomats, including me.

One of the trailblazing American diplomats I met during my Rangel professional development sessions was Ambassador Aurelia Brazeal, who taught me and my colleagues about Foreign Service writing. Serving in Micronesia, Kenya, and Ethiopia, she was the first Black woman to be appointed ambassador by three presidential administrations and the first Black woman to go from entry-level diplomat to a senior rank. Learning from Ambassador Brazeal and so many diplomats was a treat and left me grateful to the Rangel Program and the different people who invested in my professional development as a future diplomat. I thanked Ambassador Brazeal for her mentorship and legacy of excellence: she knew what she brought to the table, understood her history, and was willing to continuously mentor the next generation of American diplomats.

I pursued a career as an American diplomat because I believed that my background of having lived in different countries and cultures—speaking different languages, in combination with my desire to serve America in the context of foreign policy—all positioned me well for such work. Above all, I've been deeply grateful to the United States for the immense opportunities the country has provided me.

Tuesday, May 21, 2019, marked my first day as a U.S. congressional fellow in the office of U.S. Senator Jack Reed, who represents the state of Rhode Island. The U.S. Capitol encompasses six House and Senate buildings, including the Senate Hart Building, which housed Senator Reed's office, along with those of forty-nine other senators.

For ten weeks, I learned about the role of Congress in U.S. foreign policy. At the same time, I participated in the Rangel Program's own curriculum of professional development, which included thirty-five presentations and activities, ten site visits, and more than ninety speakers, ranging from entry-level American diplomats to U.S. ambassadors and members of Congress.

On my first day as a congressional fellow, I met Senator Reed, who at that point had served in Congress since 1997 and was a leader of the Armed Services Committee. Senator Reed welcomed me into his office, and we chatted as if we had known one another for a while. We mostly talked about our families, and I also asked him about how it felt to be a U.S. senator. He reflected that when he was first elected to the Senate, people were proud of him, but that sentiment gradually faded. In his tone, I sensed that the office and its many responsibilities had put a heavy weight on him: the endless decision-making; the loneliness; the claims on his attention from his voters, his colleagues, and many other U.S. agencies; and the issues of Rhode Island, the country, and the world. His career as a senator meant that he was always on the clock, and his time was not really his own but belonged to the American people in general and especially the people of Rhode Island. After about fifteen minutes, we wrapped up our conversation, as he told me about the many places I should visit in Washington, including the White House. I knew I was in the right office for my internship.

On the walls of his conference room, there were framed photos of people he had met during his decades of public service: presidents, celebrities, and members of Congress. Pointing at a picture of him and another man standing together and smiling, he asked me, "Do you know this guy?" I said, "It's Congressman Rangel; he looks young in this picture." The senator joked, "I looked young there too; I had black hair." We smiled. He talked about being a friend of Congressman Rangel and appreciating his service to the United States. The fellowship that brought me to Senator Reed's office was named after Congressman Rangel, who served in the U.S. House of Representatives for forty-six years, representing five different New York districts from 1971 to 2017, when he retired. I met him that summer through the Rangel Program. What struck me the most about him was his optimistic outlook on life and youthful energy at eighty-nine years old. When I asked him for advice, he said something to the effect of "Never hold a grudge against anyone because life is too short for that."

My sense that I had a good home for my internship proved right. Senator Reed and his staff were immensely cordial and helpful to me. I started my congressional internship drained from years of studying and family and professional responsibilities and didn't think that I had much energy left in me to bring to my work. But I surprised myself by taking on the challenge anyway, showing up with a positive attitude and a desire to make a contribution. And I did!

On Fridays, I took a three-hour bus trip to Philadelphia to stay with my husband and children for the weekend and help with our household responsibilities. On Sunday afternoons, I was back on a bus to DC, where I stayed in a three-bedroom dorm at Howard University that I shared with two other Rangel Fellows. Every Sunday night, I researched the various hearings scheduled in Congress and planned my week around all the ones I wanted to attend. I coordinated my weekly activities in the office and in Congress with my two supervisors. My work in Congress involved a lot of thinking, a lot of writing, a lot of learning, a lot of engagements, and very little time to process everything that I was experiencing.

One of the diplomats I met that summer had just retired after decades of service. One day in late June 2019, I was working at my desk in Senator Reed's office when my lead supervisor walked up to me and asked, "Would you be interested in meeting a former U.S. ambassador to Senegal?" I responded with a smile, "Yes, I would be interested. Absolutely!" She said she couldn't promise that the meeting would take place but would get back to me. I reflected, with gratitude, that I barely knew my supervisor, but she was already helping me grow in my future profession.

A few days later, I received an email from my supervisor that the former U.S. ambassador to Senegal had agreed to meet with me. She shared the ambassador's email with me and said I could follow up with him to request a meeting. I learned that it was Ambassador James Zumwalt, who was a retired thirty-six-year veteran of the Foreign Service and specialist in East Asia. His last diplomatic post, from 2015 to 2017, had been as U.S. ambassador to Senegal.

It was eight thirty in the morning one Tuesday in early July 2019 when I met Ambassador Zumwalt at the Bourbon Coffee in Washington. The golden rays of the sun brightened the start of the day; people walked up and down the streets as we settled outside of the café, taking in fresh air. What struck me first was how humble Ambassador Zumwalt was. He bought and served me orange juice and shared his experiences working as a diplomat. He talked about his different positions in U.S. diplomacy, from working as a first-tour diplomat in Kinshasa to his time as the deputy chief of mission in Tokyo and leading the U.S. Embassy in Dakar. He said he enjoyed his time in Senegal and found the Senegalese people to be welcoming. Inquisitive and relaxed, Ambassador Zumwalt asked me about my personal and professional background, my experiences as a Rangel Fellow, and my interest in the Foreign Service. At the time, I was considering interning in the U.S. Embassy in either Rwanda, Ghana, or Ethiopia for the summer of 2020 as part of my Rangel Graduate Fellowship Program. However, during that meeting, Ambassador Zumwalt convinced me that I could make more meaningful contributions to the embassy team in Dakar, especially because I spoke Pulaar and Wolof in addition to French and understood Senegalese culture. The following year, during another meeting I had with Ambassador Zumwalt, he told me, "You seem to be a goal-oriented person." To which I responded, "I am." He said, "You will make a great Foreign Service Officer. The Foreign Service will be lucky to have you." I later learned that the Foreign Service career required the skills of being disciplined, organized, focused, and flexible.

The Rangel Program ended up securing me an internship in the U.S. Embassy in Dakar, but soon the COVID-19 pandemic stood in the way of those plans, so I didn't intern in Senegal and did a virtual training in U.S. diplomacy instead. Nevertheless, my meeting with Ambassador Zumwalt had a major effect on my career, and the way I met him felt both strange and right. I had never met my supervisor's husband, who connected me with the ambassador and who, I later learned, worked as a civil servant in the U.S. Department of State. Though he didn't know me at all before our first meeting, Ambassador Zumwalt gave me an hour of his time and insights, which provided me with so much more clarity about U.S. diplomacy and specifically about my future career plans. I walked away grateful to have people like my supervisor and her husband speak on my behalf in rooms that I had yet to enter and to mentors who could make a tangible difference in my life.

Ambassador Zumwalt has remained an important counselor in my diplomatic career. For my first diplomatic assignment, he advised me to prioritize serving in a Portuguese-speaking country; learning this language would be valuable to my diplomatic career as few people spoke it in the Foreign Service. He also encouraged me to take care of my mental and physical health because a diplomatic career included major changes, such as long, intense hours of learning a new language and uprooting your entire life to move to different countries. I consider

Ambassador Zumwalt one of the people God sent my way to guide me on my path. A pattern that I've noticed in my life is that God, at the right time for the right reasons, has put me in touch with people who have supported me in ways that I couldn't have planned for or even imagined.

Reflecting on my internship, I feel I was extensively exposed to the operation of Congress, the legislative process, and U.S. diplomacy through the experiences of diplomats, and was very satisfied with the firsthand knowledge I gained. I learned that the Senate and House floors are spaces that require different but equally strict processes for the admission of nonpermanent congressional staff members. In addition to viewing legislative processes on the Senate floor and from the House Gallery, I went to public hearings, briefings, training sessions, and other activities that taught me much about the operations of Congress.

With my congressional engagements both in the Senate and the House, I gained a much deeper understanding of the role of Congress in foreign policy. I witnessed a variety of issues discussed and/or acted upon in the Senate and the House, including debates on education from elementary school to university, the U.S.–Mexico border migration crisis, reparations for slavery, and religious freedom.

When I started my fellowship, I requested from my supervisor that I spend time on the Senate floor to observe policymaking in action. On Wednesday, June 19, 2019, at 5:37 p.m., Senator Reed, speaking on the Senate floor and recorded live on C-SPAN, his words entered permanently into the *Congressional Record*, asked permission for another fellow in his office and me to have access to the floor. Senator Reed said, "I also ask unanimous consent that another fellow in my office, Aminata Sy, be granted the privilege of the floor until August 2, 2019." The Senate presiding officer responded, "Without objection." I watched that C-SPAN video the same day and was impressed by the transparency of that process and the fact that a U.S. senator spoke my name in one of the most powerful institutions in America and the world, so I could learn more about our country's democracy and its connection to our diplomacy.

The next morning, I got the *Congressional Record* reporting all the activities of the Senate and House on June 19, 2019, including my own admission to the Senate floor. With my supervisor, I went on the Senate floor for the first time on June 26, 2019. She taught me how to enter the floor; where to sit; what to avoid, such as bringing my phone into the chamber; and the different roles of the people who worked there. I went on to spend about five to ten hours per week on the Senate floor, watching the making and remaking of America's democracy in real time.

The Senate has a look and rhythm of its own. A royal-blue rug covers the floor; a hundred mahogany desks, organized in a semicircular shape, fill the space. A long rectangular marble desk is placed front and center of the room with a dark brown desk behind it where the presiding officer of the Senate sits. On one side of this desk hangs an American flag and on the other side hangs the flag of the Senate. Behind it hangs a royal-blue velour-like curtain, above which is a cornice enshrining the words *E pluribus unum*, meaning "Out of many, one."

On the Senate floor, I usually sat toward one side, at the back of the room on a long red seat for staff near a door. A staff member stood by that door to make sure people followed the chamber's rules—for example, the prohibition on using phones on the floor. High schoolers (girls and boys aged sixteen and older) served as Senate pages. They dressed in navy blue uniforms, white dress shirts, and black shoes and helped with different tasks, like setting up the desks before senators spoke, bringing them papers and water, and collecting their statements for the records. Stenographers stood near senators as they spoke and typed every word, rotating in ten-minute shifts. By the following morning, all the Senate floor activities were published in the *Congressional Record*. About six staff members sat in a row in front of the floor and called the roll as senators voted, the staffers' voices echoing throughout the room. The chamber was the busiest during the voting period; senators came in and out to cast their votes and chatted among themselves.

The majestic and dignified architecture of the room conveyed that democracy was a serious and artistic process that needed the diplomacy, individuality, and collectivity of the people involved in it. There was a sense of precise routine and cadence in the Senate's activities but also of constant change. Every issue debated, every statement a senator made, every vote, the presence or absence of members—each altered the scene and outcome in some way, small or large. Big issues involving the livelihood and well-being of the American public and beyond were at stake, as well as billions of dollars and powerful and powerless stakeholders. Every bill that passed the Senate created a precedent for future legislation. U.S. democracy was this dynamic mix of slow and steady movement, with short- and long-term consequences for institutions and millions of people, in America and around the world. It's on that same floor that senators debated, agreed, disagreed, and compromised on a range of issues, including migration, which was front and center in the Senate that summer.

I attended anywhere from seven to fifteen engagements per week in the U.S. Congress, most of them public hearings hosted by different committees in the House and Senate on major issues impacting the United States and the world.

The legislative process requires that members work together: they must advocate for an issue to colleagues, the American public, and other stakeholders; debate; conduct public hearings; craft a bill and incorporate amendments; pass it in both the Senate and House; and send it to the president for signature or veto. And this is a simplified version of the process.

I attended and or watched many public hearings in Congress. One hearing, titled "Educating Our Educators: How Federal Policy Can Better Support Teachers and School Leaders," addressed the growing gap between America's diverse student body and its corps of teachers, who presently don't reflect this diversity and are not trained to meet learners' needs.

This hearing reminded me of my experiences as a parent in the School District of Philadelphia and how many factors could threaten a child's education: a teacher's cultural incompetence, a shortage of teachers and frequent turnovers, an unsettling classroom and school climate, and lack of homework support and resources. I testified three times in front of Philadelphia's public and elected officials concerning some of these issues in public schools, namely, the need to provide greater access to quality prekindergarten programs, the struggles faced by students in the African diaspora, unsafe learning environments, lack of homework support, and teacher shortage.

In my testimony on May 25, 2017, to the Philadelphia School Reform Commission, which included the superintendent, I said, "Cultural diversity without inclusion is meaningless." Why? Because as a parent volunteer for years in the School District of Philadelphia, including in my son Ibra's public school in West Philadelphia, I witnessed too many African diaspora students and immigrant learners without English language or homework support. When their parents dropped them off in the morning, they were often crying, because they didn't want to stay in a learning environment where they couldn't talk to anyone. I consoled some of these students and supported them in reading, writing, and speaking English and in completing their assignments. I translated the teacher's report card notations from English to French so that French-speaking immigrant parents could understand them.

The two biggest gaps that I noticed were linguistic and cultural. First, teachers did not share a common language with English learners that the latter could use while learning English.

Because I speak Pulaar, Wolof, and French, I was able to support some students in learning English, but the classroom teachers were rarely so equipped. Second, the differences in culture between English learners and their teachers created another barrier. For example, in many African cultures, including Senegal, where I grew up, it's a sign of respect for children to look down when an adult is talking to them. But in American culture, adults expect a child to look them directly in the eye when they speak; otherwise, the child can be seen as disrespectful, dismissive, or untrustworthy. It takes many African immigrant students years of living in America to get used to looking teachers in the eye. These cultural differences play out in the classroom and create tension between students and their teachers.

The congressional hearing on "Educating Our Educators" was a reminder of how far the U.S. education system has come and how far it still needs to go to teach an ever-changing population. The superintendent of education for the state of Louisiana was among the speakers at this hearing and stated, "We owe it to teachers and to their students to prepare them in a professional manner and to declare them effective before they take a full-time job as a classroom teacher."

The more prepared and supported teachers are for diverse classrooms, the more they'll be able to deliver a life-changing education for children, no matter their backgrounds. Our democracy and the future of the United States in part depend on recruiting, training, retaining, and supporting a teaching workforce that reflects the richness of every child who walks into a classroom.

Though the congressional hearings addressed serious issues that impacted domestic and international affairs, there was an aspect of these proceedings that came across as a show made for television. The witnesses were placed front and center, with Democrats seated on one side and Republicans on the other, while public attendees assembled at the back of the room. Photographers, videographers, reporters, and congressional staffers were scattered throughout the room, each focused on their roles. The line of questioning; the selection of the witnesses;

the interactions among congressional members; the decorum, rules, and mannerisms during hearings all seemed so precise yet appeared natural. I imagined that a sociologist could write a thesis simply on the interactions and configurations in those congressional rooms and their meaning to power and policy-making. Power revealed itself in those hearing rooms not just in what was done but in how it was done. For instance, who spoke, when they spoke, and for how long.

During the summer of 2019, Congress was grappling with the U.S.–Mexico border crisis. When migrants crossed the border, many parents and their children were separated due to U.S. policy. Many migrants died either on their way to the border or once in U.S. custody, where they were packed into overcrowded facilities. Reports revealed that migrants were not getting three meals a day and lacked basic hygiene requirements like toothbrushes and soap. U.S. border agents couldn't manage the overwhelming flow of migrants.

I attended a public hearing in the U.S. Senate titled "Unprecedented Migration at the U.S. Southern Border: The Exploitation of Migrants Through Smuggling, Trafficking, and Involuntary Servitude." The chairing senator characterized the conditions at the border as "horrific" and described a chilling photo of a father, Oscar Ramírez, and his twenty-three-month-old daughter, Valeria, both floating face down in the Rio Grande; they had drowned trying to cross from Mexico into the U.S. The image captured the price that migrants paid in search of a better life in the United States and exposed the policies that led to such disasters. The photo put human faces to the horrors of the migrants' plight at the border and made clear that the issue wasn't a mere political debate but one of life and death.

In July 2019, I also watched a hearing in the U.S. House titled "Kids in Cages: Inhumane Treatment at the Border." In it, Yazmin Juárez, a Guatemalan migrant, talked about the death of her nineteen-month-old child, Mariee, while in U.S. Immigration and Customs Enforcement (ICE) detention and her desire to help other migrant children in memory of her daughter. Juárez spoke in Spanish, and the translator sitting by her side translated her message. In a trembling voice, holding back her tears, Juárez said that the United States is a country of opportunity, for work, healthcare, and freedom. That's why she wanted to bring her child to the United States, to have access to those opportunities that she didn't have in her home country. She said, "ICE detention centers are terrible, inadequate places to lock children up, I am sorry to say as if they were animals." At one point in the hearing, Juárez broke down in tears explaining how hard it was for her to get up every day because she had lived and worked for her daughter Mariee, who wasn't alive anymore. Another congresswoman described the migrants' conditions in U.S. custody as "human rights abuses" and apologized to Juárez, saying, "As a mom, as an American, and as a human being, I am sorry, I am so very sorry that we have failed you." On July 1, 2019, the U.S. Congress passed the Emergency Supplemental Appropriations for Humanitarian Assistance and Security at the Southern Border Act to address many of the problems related to the migrants' situation.

There were days during my time in Congress when I felt like a brick was sitting on my heart, stopping me from breathing and functioning properly. The hearings about the suffering of migrants at the U.S.–Mexico border were some of those days. I was reconfirmed in my belief that policy is about people's lives and how those lives will turn out; policy is about raw emotions; policy is about life and death.

Through research and writing in support of Senator Reed's senior policy advisor on education, I made contributions to education policy for the state of Rhode Island and beyond, especially for immigrants and English learners. I learned from research on the Rhode Island immigrant population at the time that one in eight people in the state were immigrants and one in seven were first-generation Americans. The majority of the Rhode Island immigrant population seemed well integrated into American society in terms of speaking English. Immigrants contributed millions to the state's economy, regardless of their legal status. However, many English language learners in the state's public schools had not met English proficiency standards. In the context of K–12 education, my recommendations included that educators know the population they serve, so they can better teach them, and that the state should adopt culturally responsive curricula and train teachers to become culturally competent. I also conducted research on access to higher education to contribute to the amendment of a bill on the subject introduced by the House.

Though my time as a congressional fellow was brief, my experiences in Congress were deep enough that I started to navigate the place with confidence. One afternoon on the steps of the U.S. Capitol, I chatted with a congressional guard about his work and mine. He said to me with such certainty, "You will be our ambassador, and you're going to represent us around the world so well." One Saturday, I gave my husband and children a tour of the Capitol, the Senate, and the office of Senator Reed and watched my kids run around the Senate Hart Building as if it were their playground. I toured the House floor with my supervisor through my connection with a guard and she said to me, "I've been here for over twenty years and didn't get on the House floor; it only took you six weeks to do it." The fast pace of congressional activity, my closeness to processes that I had imagined and some that I had never imagined, my contacts with the people who shape the direction of our country and the world every day, my own day-to-day role in that work, all felt like both a dream and reality.

On August 1, 2019, Senator Reed and his staff gathered in the office's conference room for a farewell event, complete with a cake and sweet drinks, for me and another staffer. The senator thanked me for my contributions to the office, and I thanked him for his service to our country. Then he handed me a beautifully framed and autographed photo of me and him and a handwritten thank-you note. The senator's chief of staff told me, "You're going to be a great diplomat." As we walked out of the farewell event, the office manager said to me, "They like you here!" I responded, "I like them too!" We shared a smile, and I headed back to my desk. I felt a mix of profound joy and pride.

I left my internship with a much greater appreciation of Congress's influence on U.S. foreign policy and therefore on the Department of State and the Foreign Service, and overall, I became more informed and prepared to serve as a U.S. diplomat. I also better appreciated Congress's role as the overseer of the executive branch and the grave responsibility pressing on congressional members and their staff as they juggle local, national, and international issues. Even with the many problems our country and the world faced and the polarization of

U.S. politics, I left Congress more hopeful about America's future and even more committed to serving my country.

Chapter Eight

Resilience in Adversity

"WHAT YOU'RE TRYING TO DO IS HERCULEAN." THOSE WERE the words of my academic advisor during my first days, in August 2019, at American University (AU), where I was pursuing a master's degree in public policy with a concentration in international development. She meant that I was setting myself up to fail at the university. I had told her that I decided to commute over 130 miles between my home in Philadelphia and Washington, DC, where AU is located, to attend classes. And she said that previous students who attempted to commute such long distances ended up dropping out, so I should find somewhere to live in DC while studying or postpone my education until I could do so. What my academic advisor didn't know was the long and difficult journey that had brought me to that point, that nothing and no one was going to stop me from continuing my education, and that it wasn't just about getting a master's degree but about getting myself and my family out of poverty, about starting a new chapter in our lives—and also about serving the United States.

I chose to serve America by pursuing a career in U.S. diplomacy through the Rangel Graduate Fellowship Program. The fellowship not only placed me in a congressional internship but also helped pay for my graduate studies, gave me my first training in diplomacy, and arranged for my employment with the U.S. Foreign Service.

America is the country where I've built and lived my life with my husband since the age of twenty-one. I gave birth to my three children in America. I returned to school and earned degrees in America. I explored different careers in America. I've grown into a mature human being in America. I've experienced opportunities that I never imagined before in America. So America means a great deal to me, not because it's flawless, but because it's a country that has given me and millions of immigrants a space and a chance to become. I have a strong desire to give back to the country that has given me so much.

As a Rangel Fellow, I had to pursue a master's degree program relevant to U.S. diplomacy and maintain a minimum grade point average of 3.2 as a full-time student throughout the two-year duration of my studies. Otherwise, I risked losing not only the fellowship but my potential future appointment as a diplomat and would have to repay the U.S. Department of State for the portion of my fellowship it had subsidized.

In selecting which programs to apply to, I focused on three priorities. The university had to have a public policy program, provide enough financial support so I could avoid student debt, and be close enough to my home in Philadelphia so I could commute to and from the school and not live on campus or near it. The Rangel Graduate Fellowship Program partnered with many U.S. universities that offered programs in government and diplomacy, but most did not meet all three of my criteria. Harvard's Kennedy School of Government, for example, was among the dozens of schools that reached out to me, encouraging me to apply to their programs, but I declined because I couldn't commute back and forth to Cambridge, Massachusetts.

Above all, I prioritized my family's stability as I pursued a master's degree. My husband remained the sole breadwinner of our household, and he continued working from 5:00 a.m. to 1:00 p.m., Monday through Friday. So I continued to get our children ready for school in the morning, drive them to school, help with their homework, and follow their academic progress. I couldn't live in another city for two years to study for my master's degree; I had to take care of my family and go to school at the same time. In the end, AU satisfied all of my three criteria: it had an excellent program in public policy, its distance from Philadelphia of over 130 miles was commutable, and it offered me a scholarship to supplement the Rangel Graduate Fellowship funding.

My bus trip from Philadelphia to Washington, DC, and back to Philadelphia the same day remained a key struggle while studying at AU. During my first semester, in the fall of 2019, I enrolled in three courses—economics (Mondays, 2:30 p.m. to 5:20 p.m.), statistics (Mondays, 5:30 p.m. to 8:00 p.m.), and foundations of policy (Wednesdays, 5:30 p.m. to 8:00 p.m.)—and that meant a grueling commute two days a week.

From Monday to Friday, I started my days at 5:00 a.m. For instance, on Mondays, after getting my kids off to school, I drove to a Philadelphia Center City parking lot, parked my car there, and walked for about five minutes to a bus station, where I caught the bus to Washington, DC. The bus departed for DC at 8:30 a.m. and arrived there at Union Station at 11:20 a.m. I caught a metro and arrived at the Tenleytown stop near AU at around 12:30 p.m. Then I waited for about ten to fifteen minutes for the AU bus that would take me to campus, where I finally arrived at around 1:00 p.m. I asked my statistics professor's permission to leave class at 7:45 p.m. on Mondays, hurried to Union Station to depart DC at 8:30 p.m., arrived back in Philadelphia at 11:50 p.m. or midnight, walked to get my car from the parking lot, and drove home. I got home at around 12:30 a.m., slept for a few hours, then woke up to prepare my children for school. I easily spent ten to eleven hours a week commuting to and from AU, and that was assuming that the buses and metros ran on schedule, which they did not always do. I told my husband often that I didn't know how I would sustain my commuting routine for two years.

I engaged in a monologue in my head as I hopped onto the bus to travel to AU.

What am I doing? Who does this? How is this normal? I'm traveling from one city to another to go to school and return home the same day? That's crazy. I repeated this to myself for about three months every time I got on the bus to go to school. Every time I undertook that commute, I had to convince myself that it was worth doing. But eventually, my internal monologue changed: *I'm just going to school. I'll return home tonight. That's okay.*

I learned to eat and drink just enough so that I could withstand my time on the bus without using the restroom. I learned to manage the nausea that came over me on the bus, to tolerate the smell of cleaning products that I could taste in my mouth, to bear with the noises of the road that rang in my ears long after I arrived home, to sit next to strangers for hours, to brave the darkness of the nights when returning to Philadelphia, to study in buses and metros, to carry on despite my sore body and fatigue from extensive hours of sitting, to pray that I'd get home safe. I almost never slept on the bus but always took a scarf with me and sometimes covered my face with it and closed my eyes for about thirty minutes to recharge.

Students and professors at the school who learned about my long commute couldn't believe it at first. Every time I arrived on campus, I felt a sense of accomplishment. Before starting my weekly conference with one of my professors, she would ask, "How are you, Aminata? How was the commute?" I would respond with a big smile, "I'm here; I made it." A few of my classmates even offered to let me stay at their homes near AU when there was inclement weather. I prayed that I wouldn't need that kind of support, and I never did. I just wanted to attend my classes and go home.

I also struggled academically. Over the years, I developed study skills, determination, and resourcefulness that allowed me to push through and improve even when I experienced difficulties with some courses. For one thing, at Community College of Philadelphia and at the University of Pennsylvania, I was on campus enough to get the help I needed. But at AU, I spent too little time on campus to get the necessary support, so I couldn't afford to fall behind in my learning.

Statistics and economics were both difficult subjects for me, and I was taking both for the first time in my academic career.

I made appointments with my professors before class to get help and also attended some statistics tutoring sessions. In the end, I improved in my economics course and finished it with an A-minus, but I remained lost in statistics, completing the class with a C. My overall grade point average that first semester stood at 3.0, below the minimum of 3.2 that the Rangel Graduate Fellowship Program required. In February 2020, I received a letter from the Rangel Graduate Fellowship Program stating that they had put me on academic probation and requesting that I take immediate steps to improve my academic performance for my second semester and provide a plan with concrete steps to raise my grade point average.

Without their prompting, I had already committed to improving my academics and maintaining that momentum. I started taking steps to improve my grades during the spring semester of 2020. Before classes began, I had reached out to all three of my professors and asked for their syllabi, so I could prepare for the semester in terms of academic requirements, office hour conferences, and my Philadelphia–DC commute. However, the challenge remained to sustain my efforts day in and day out, week in and week out.

For that entire semester, I booked weekly meetings with two professors and biweekly meetings with another and scheduled weekly tutoring sessions to get support for my second statistics course. I also booked weekly Philadelphia–DC bus trips, which helped me stay on track with showing up to every class. I remained in close contact with my professors and tutor to follow up on assignments, questions, feedback, and scheduling. I organized my calendar with all of my assignments' deadlines for the semester and centered my weekly activities around school and family. I outlined my daily academic tasks, executed them, and met all deadlines. I participated in class discussions and asked questions for clarification and in two of my classes led group projects, with papers and presentations as deliverables. I met with my professors and teammates to discuss our group projects and remained in ongoing communication with them as the projects progressed.

However, starting in March 2020, the world drastically changed with the onset of the global COVID-19 pandemic, an airborne disease. To reduce people's risk of exposure to COVID-19, AU announced that it was temporarily canceling its in-person classes and moving them online and soon did so permanently for the remainder of that semester and my subsequent time at the university. For me, that meant a pause in my Philadelphia–DC commutes and taking classes online for the first time in my academic career.

By that point, COVID-19, which had started in Wuhan, China, about two months prior, had spread to more than sixty countries, including the United States, and led to an all-out public panic: whole nations in effect shut down, canceling major activities involving crowds, and thousands of people died or got sick. I had never seen a disease simultaneously create such panic at the local, national, and international levels. There was a sense that no one was safe, regardless of their geographic location or socioeconomic status. Overnight, U.S. university students had to vacate their dorms and figure out where to live for the remainder of the semester. I received emails from my three AU professors, each explaining how we would conduct classes online. Every day felt more uncertain and overwhelming than the previous one. The COVID-19 pandemic stopped the world from going about business as usual and gave globalization a whole new meaning: around the world, people's regular routines were collectively uprooted, and no one knew what to expect next.

Schools also closed throughout Philadelphia and the country, transitioning to virtual education, so my children were all learning from home. For the next three months, I became Ibra's second-grade teacher, from March to May 2020, when his school year ended. Ibra's teacher emailed me his daily lessons by 9:00 a.m., and we sat together at our dining room table, where I taught him math, language arts, science, and social studies until around noon. His lessons were organized by themes depending on the day of the week: Musical Monday, Terrific Tuesday, Workout Wednesday, Think-About-It Thursday or Throwback Thursday, and Fun-Day Friday. Every Friday, I took pictures of all of Ibra's completed work and emailed them to his teacher for grading.

I spent much more time with Ibra during those three months than I normally would and enjoyed engaging in his daily progress. Whether helping him present a report on the planet Neptune, playing spelling games, reading stories, or taking him outside to ride his bike or play basketball, I was grateful for this chance to spend more time with him and for the memories it left me with. Our studying also involved engaging in silly salsa ballroom dancing to move our bodies and a daily exercise of writing out times tables. By the end of that period, Ibra had written his times tables from two to twelve, filling up his composition book. "I wrote all of this, mommy," Ibra said. "Yes, you did," I replied. "You can do many things when you focus. I'm proud of you! Are you proud of yourself?"

"Yes!" Ibra said, nodding with a smile. Sometimes, he cooked fried eggs for breakfast and said, "I'm Chef Ibra." Many times, we shared laughs during his lessons; I marveled as I watched him just being a child in the midst of the madness of the pandemic. Ibra wrote me a thank-you note on our last day of class. "Thank you for being my teacher for the rest of the school year and for being there for me. Also thank you for being the best you can!"

Ibra would often ask how I was still a student at my age, and I would respond that I would take him around the world when I completed my studies. "How are you going to do that when you don't even have any money?" he would ask. "That's why I'm going to school, to get a job," I would say. "Remember, you're going to be my traveling buddy. We'll go around the world together!"

Meanwhile, I was learning how to learn virtually. That spring semester of 2020, I took three courses: foreign aid, project management, and statistics. Among my assignments, I led, prepared, and presented, all in online formats, a group project in my foreign aid class and in my project management course. I produced a plan for drafting a three-year report about ACLP's work, a plan which I later implemented. Every week, I met virtually with my statistics professor, who explained the concepts well, so I remained on track with the subject. Through each week, I moved from one task to the next, feeling breathless from my numerous commitments at home and in my graduate program, from Ibra's schooling, from the barrage of emails from AU, and from the constant news—online, on television, on social media—of death and suffering connected to COVID-19…all coming at me at once.

I savored the moments of break, when my family and I spent time together, just enjoying one another's company. I remember a sunny Saturday afternoon at Clark Park in West Philadelphia when I played Frisbee, tag, and basketball with Ibra, then eight years old, and Aissata, sixteen. As in old times, Aissata asked me to carry her on my back, and I did, but not for long. "I can't do this anymore, baby girl, you are too heavy for me now," I told her. She also wanted to carry me on her back, so I went along with it. I hopped on Aissata's back, and she walked to our car parked nearby. It seemed that she might drop me at any point as I laughed all the way to the car. "It actually doesn't feel bad carrying you, Mommy," Aissata said. "Now you know that you can carry your mom on your back," I responded. "It's not fair. You had three kids, and you're still not that heavy," Aissata remarked.

The news of change continued. I had originally planned to spend my Rangel Graduate Fellowship overseas internship in the U.S. Embassy in Dakar during the summer of 2020, but for weeks, I was unsure whether or not the program would carry on with its overseas internships during the pandemic. In April 2020, I received the answer via an email written in bold red font: "This is an urgent notification to inform you that, due to the COVID-19 pandemic, the U.S. Department of State has replaced all summer 2020 travel planned for Pickering and Rangel Fellows with virtual programming." In many ways, that decision was disappointing. I had looked forward so much to working for ten weeks in a U.S. Embassy, representing the United States, in Dakar, the city I grew up in. That was a surreal thought! My younger self could never have imagined such a turn of events.

Still, the cancellation of the overseas internship had a bright side, and I chose to focus on it. I took an online class during the summer of 2020 that would reduce my course load for the coming academic year from seven to six, meaning that I could take three courses in fall 2020 and three in spring 2021 and therefore complete my program with less stress. Even so, expectations—family, academic, and professional—weighed on me constantly; it felt like I was climbing a mountain while someone tugged downward on one of my legs, so I was always in danger of falling off or balancing on a thin rope from which I could fall off at any time. But I kept pressing forward. My family's future depended on my educational and career outcomes. I started to see the end of my long educational journey and the beginning of a career as an American diplomat. I thanked God for giving me the heart, courage, and tenacity to keep going.

Starting in May of 2020, social unrest erupted around the United States and the world as images of the murder of George Floyd, a Black American, flooded social media and television screens. Our neighborhood in West Philadelphia, especially our block at 52nd and Walnut Streets, became a place of ongoing protests and looting that played out live on local, national, and international news outlets. Military officers from the National Guard and their tanks were stationed along 52nd and Walnut Streets, while police officers maintained a massive presence, and the loud whirring of news helicopters over our homes became the background "music" of our days. The city imposed a 6:00 p.m. to 6:00 a.m. curfew; dozens of people were arrested; our neighborhood seemed like a war zone. The reality out in our streets seemed a grim contrast to my academic and professional worlds, which I accessed through AU online learning and the Rangel Graduate Fellowship virtual internship.

On a sunny day in early June 2020, I marched in Center City with my children alongside other Philadelphians in a peaceful protest. We marched because the lives of Black people in America are not yet fully valued; because America can and must do better by its Black citizens; because the traumas of injustice that Black people face in the country permeate across generations; because every human being, every child deserves to live with dignity, in peace and safety. During that march, we kneeled for eight minutes and forty-six seconds in solidarity with George Floyd's agony. That was how long the police officer kneeled on his neck as he cried, "I can't breathe" and then died.

For me, joining a peaceful protest, talking to my children about the social unrest around us, and writing down my thoughts about the situation were ways to process the overwhelmingly painful emotions that I felt as a human being, a parent, and a citizen who yearned for an America that would treat its Black citizens as valuable human beings. I went through a week where I couldn't process anything that I learned in my summer course or my internship and couldn't sleep well. I was always thinking about the safety of my family and that of Black people around the country.

Another way I processed my thoughts and feelings was by starting to exercise daily to remain mentally, emotionally, and physically strong and healthy. At Clark Park in West Philadelphia, every morning from Monday to Friday, from around 7:30 a.m. to 8:30 a.m., I walked, ran, stretched, and reflected on my days. No matter the weather or how I felt on any given day,

I still showed up to exercise and take in the beauty of nature. My body used to ache all the time; not anymore. My mind used to feel overclouded; not anymore. My walking speed had slowed down; not anymore. My endurance for exercise had declined; not anymore. I walked alone but knew that God always accompanied me, as in the many other lonely journeys that I had taken in my life.

One morning, I wept with joy as I walked into Clark Park. I cried because of the pain and sacrifices that had brought me to that point in my life. I cried because of the hours, days, weeks, months, and years of effort that I had put in to get there. I cried because of the loneliness of the years of studying and the very high level of discipline the journey demanded. I cried because I was close to earning a master's degree, even though I started out as a low-income, non-English speaker in America and was a first-generation college student throughout my studies. I cried because God created a path for me that I could never have imagined for myself. I cried because there were many times when I felt like quitting but kept going. I cried because I was extremely grateful for my journey and for all the blessings God had given me from the time I was born to that very day. I thanked God and prayed that he would continue to give me the courage to push through on the hard days and to rejoice in the good ones.

As the unrest raged in our neighborhood and around our country, I regrouped my energies and dove back into my academic and professional commitments. I learned virtually from so many giants of U.S. diplomacy that summer of 2020, including Ambassador Tulinabo Mushingi, who was serving as U.S. Ambassador to Senegal, and to Guinea Bissau at the time, and who had immigrated to America from the Democratic Republic of Congo. He joined the Foreign Service in 1993 and is the first native African to serve as a U.S. ambassador to an African country.

I wrote a note to Ambassador Mushingi on behalf of our Rangel Graduate Fellowship cohort, thanking him for sharing with us his approach to diplomacy and his many insights into the operations of U.S. embassies. I had followed Ambassador Mushingi's work through the social media site of the U.S. Embassy in Dakar and admired his diplomacy style—a blend of empathy, humility, and respect in interacting with people, in this case, Senegalese. For example, when Ambassador Mushingi visited a school for blind children, he put on a blindfold to walk in the shoes of learners, and in another instance, he prepared and served *ngalakh,* a sweet Senegalese millet porridge flavored with peanut butter, to people residing and working near the U.S. Embassy in Dakar. In many ways, he embodied the kind of diplomat I wanted to be by reflecting the best of what America had to offer to the world.

I acquired many new skills in my internship and at AU, completing the rest of my courses online because of the ongoing pandemic. I learned how to analyze big policy issues, such as those affecting education, and how to write and present policy documents in a clear and concise way. I worked with three other AU classmates on a paper on K–12 education policy in the United States, titled "Culturally Responsive Teaching Practices for Immigrant Students and English Learners in Public Schools." The paper was based on ACLP's teaching practices and also drew from studies in the United States, Finland, and Norway. I shared that paper with the Philadelphia mayor, leaders in the School District of Philadelphia, and the senior staff of Senator Reed.

I was nominated for an AU award for Outstanding Scholarship at the Graduate Level. One of my nominators, a professor who had taught me two courses at AU, one on project management and one on public–private partnership, wrote, "While I have had the privilege of teaching many outstanding students during my AU career, I can think of no student who has made a greater impression or impact, nor who is more deserving of this high University honor, than Aminata—a true AU Changemaker!" I graduated from AU with a master's degree in public policy on May 8, 2021, sharing the momentous occasion with my family and feeling deep gratitude. My mom had never gone past the third grade in her schooling, my grandmother had never gone to school at all, nor had my aunt who raised me, but here I was graduating with a master's degree.

That day, I completed my program at AU, which marked the end of my eleven-year academic journey as an adult, starting from my GED in 2010 to my master's degree in 2021. Below is the message I wrote on the social media platform LinkedIn that day.

> From a high school dropout to a master's degree to American diplomacy.
>
> To God, thank you for taking care of me throughout my life.
>
> To my parents, thank you for bringing me into this world.
>
> To my husband and children, thank you for your unshakable love and support.
>
> To my aunt, thank you for raising me and teaching me about life.

To my godmother, thank you for your generosity.

To my instructors, professors, tutors, and advisors, thank you for sharing your knowledge and resources.

To my supporters, thank you for your contributions to my journey.

To the people of Philadelphia, thank you for sharing our city with my family and me.

To the many institutions that educated and trained me, thank you for your contributions to my academic and professional journeys.

To Senegal, thank you for providing me with a solid foundation.

To America, thank you for being a country where dreams can become a reality.

As you pursue your goals, you'll face many moments of disruption, discouragement, and disappointment, but you need to press forward, no matter what. Take a short break if you need to, reflect if you need to, cry if you need to, and talk to someone if you need to. Then keep going. To make extensive progress in life, you'll have to take risks and deal with situations that seem impossible to overcome. I'm here to tell you that just about anything you can imagine, you can achieve. It won't be easy, but you can do it.

Chapter Nine

Landing a Dream Career

MY FAMILY AND I MOVED FROM PHILADELPHIA, PENNSYL-vania, to Arlington, Virginia, on July 5, 2021, and I started my Foreign Service career the following day. For months, my family and I had been packing up the years of our lives in Philadelphia, getting rid of and donating books, clothes, shoes, furniture, and dishes. The Department of State's movers picked up our things and drove them to a storage facility in the Washington area. At the same time, I was studying for my master's degree in public policy at American University, finishing it up in the middle of the COVID-19 pandemic. The few people who knew about my move asked me where I would be working, and my answer was always: "I have no idea yet." This was a confusing and almost unbelievable response for them; they knew that I would work overseas, so they thought I would be assigned to a specific country before leaving Philadelphia. How could I uproot my life and that of my family without knowing what the future held for us? I left Philadelphia with my husband, Aissata, and Ibra, clueless about where my career would take me and my family and what it would mean for us. Amadou stayed at our Philadelphia home with my mom while my husband and I figured out her caretaking situation because she still needed dialysis three times a week.

My Foreign Service orientation, known as A-100 in the Department of State, also took place during the COVID-19 pandemic, from July 6, 2021, to August 10, 2021. This meant I did my entire orientation virtually, through Zoom calls, emails, online chats, and independent study, from Monday through Friday, 8:00 a.m. to 4:00 p.m. I was up by 5:00 a.m., took a walk outdoors, and prepared for the day, completing any work assigned the previous day and logging into Zoom at around 7:50 a.m., stationed either in my bedroom or the living room of our apartment.

Our Foreign Service class was composed of 125 diplomats: 85 generalists and 40 specialists. These included men and women from a wide variety of backgrounds. I was the only immigrant from Senegal in our class and one of only five Black women.

Foreign Service generalists work in five different career tracks: political, economic, public diplomacy, management, and consular. They choose one main career focus but can be placed in positions requiring any of these areas of expertise. Foreign Service specialists focus their careers on one of the following areas: administration, building construction, operations and maintenance, information technology, English language programs, law enforcement and security, or medical and health. I entered the Foreign Service as a political officer, which is subdivided into different portfolios: human rights, internal politics, external politics, political military affairs, and international narcotics and law enforcement affairs.

On Tuesday, July 6, 2021, I was sworn in and started serving as an American diplomat. As I took my daily walk near our apartment building, I reflected on the path that had brought me to that point in my life. I was grateful to God for bringing me that far, for taking care of me and my family, for protecting us, and for showing us the way. I deeply appreciated my husband for his time and effort and for supporting me in every way.

I was pleased that my desire to help my kids propelled me to go on despite all the adversities that I had faced in my life. I just kept going, believing that my family and I deserved better than a life of mere survival. The road that led us to that day was long and hard, but one that I was very proud of. I knew and remembered my journey and my priorities; I had never forgotten that I was a wife and mother. I took life as it came, and when challenging situations unfolded, I dealt with them the best way I knew.

That day, at 10:30 a.m., I sat at my desk, attending my virtual Foreign Service swearing-in ceremony, along with other colleagues. My husband sat on the couch behind me, watching and video-recording the moment. A Department of State official administered the oath of office to all of us. These were her opening remarks:

> On behalf of the director general, I would like to welcome you to the Foreign Service as you commence your appointment with the U.S. Department of State. We very much appreciate your flexibility as the global COVID-19 pandemic has forced us to make a number

of changes to our traditional hiring, orientation, and training plans. We are especially grateful to you for your continued interest in serving your nation at the Department of State during this critical time. Today marks the end of a long journey as a candidate and the beginning of a new career… Everyone, if you can please unmute your microphone, stand and raise your right hand, and repeat after me.

Standing in front of my computer screen, I unmuted my computer, raised my right hand, and repeated: "I, Aminata Sy, do solemnly swear that I will support and defend the Constitution of the United States against all enemies, foreign and domestic; that I will bear true faith and allegiance to the same; that I take this obligation freely, without any mental reservation or purpose of evasion; and that I will well and faithfully discharge the duties of the office on which I am about to enter. So help me God."

We all muted our computers again, and the official said, "Congratulations and welcome to the Department of State!" I turned to my husband and said, "That's it." He exclaimed, "Congratulations! You did it; you deserve it. *Alhadulillahi rabbil alamin.*" (Meaning "Praise be to God.") We embraced, thanked God, and reflected. We both knew how long and how hard we had worked to finally experience that ten-minute swearing-in ceremony. My husband said, "God is never going to leave us. He'll continue to clear our path."

My children, on the other hand, were not as impressed. Amadou, who was there on a brief visit, said that because the swearing-in ceremony was virtual, it didn't seem like a big deal to him. Ibra found it strange that I stood in front of a computer screen repeating words after someone. Aissata was sound asleep. By that point, I had participated in so many virtual interactions that my swearing-in ceremony didn't stand out as extraordinary to my children. They didn't quite grasp the importance of that moment until months later when we left everything and everyone we knew to start a new life in another country.

Around 11:30 a.m. that day, I posted a message on the social media platform LinkedIn that went viral.

> Today, I was sworn in as an American diplomat to represent the United States of America around the world. As an immigrant to the United States, I cannot yet put into words what this privilege to serve means to me and the many sacrifices and years it took to achieve this dream.
>
> I am so grateful to my husband for his support and sacrifices. I am so grateful to my children for their love and motivation. I am so grateful for the contributions of many supporters and institutions.
>
> The journey continues…

I went to the courtyard of our apartment, along with my husband, to play with Ibra. All around us were tall buildings, while before us spread the recreation area: a grassy square in the center, couches, chairs, and tables, a pool, two electric barbecues, and tables where I played table tennis with Ibra. "Come on, Mommy, I'm going to beat you," Ibra said. "We'll see. Show me what you got," I responded. We played, laughed, chatted, enjoyed the fresh air and the sun, and then about forty-five minutes later caught the elevator back to our seventh-floor apartment.

I checked my LinkedIn post and saw that at least 20,000 people had already viewed it, and hundreds had left congratulatory comments. The volume and speed at which the views and comments were pouring in was something I had never experienced before, and they continued to grow by the minute. In the end, the post had 508,483 views, 13,127 likes, 1,406 comments, and 62 shares.

I also received at least 100 private messages on LinkedIn. I told my husband, "I don't know what's happening, but it's crazy." He said that so many people were proud and happy for me because I had achieved something rare for an immigrant, wife, and mother. These were mostly strangers; people from the United States and other countries; men and women across races, ages, and nationalities, with a unified message: you inspire us, and the United States is a great country for making a space for you and many other immigrants to achieve your dreams.

These were some of their comments:

> Congratulations! And I would like to learn about your path to where you are today! I'm an immigrant studying international development in graduate school. I'm hoping to work with/for the U.S. State Department one day.

> I'm a first-generation college student, daughter of immigrants, and proud community college graduate. I would love to learn about your career trajectory and experiences leading up to joining the FS [Foreign Service] as I'm interested in joining the FS in the near future.

> Inspiring. Keep pushing the limits. Wishing you the very best and much success for this journey. You are serving a great country. Your home country is also proud of you. Well, I am.

A great privilege, it is! Congratulations! Very few nations will allow immigrants to reach such a sensitive position.

I took in that day in all of its ordinary and extraordinary experiences and continued my training for my new career.

The bidding process by which new diplomats get their assignments makes the world seem small. The countries appear on a single list, and the diplomats choose from them as though selecting from a menu of different nations. Diplomats rank the countries on the list in their order of preference and talk to their career development officers about their main reasons for those choices. Then the new diplomats submit a final ranking of their assignment preferences to their career development officers along with an explanation for their selections. The career development officers make the final decision about assignments.

The list our class was given included eighty-five positions around the world for Foreign Service generalists, and I talked with my husband and children about all the possibilities. We researched the countries and shared our preferences with one another. I also sought guidance from three mentors, two retired diplomats, and one currently in the service. I made my first choices by considering my family's feedback and priorities, my career goals, my mentors' advice, and my research.

Combining all of these considerations, in the end, I chose Brasilia, Brazil. It was my top preference because I read and consistently heard from American diplomats who served in the city that it was a family-friendly place to live and work in terms of safety, tranquility, good quality of life, and decent schools. I wanted to learn Portuguese and use the language as a long-term career skill for assignments on the African continent and in other positions around the world. My six months of language training would allow Aissata to attend twelfth grade in the United States and provide some time to find a caretaker for my mom.

On August 10, 2021, I learned my first diplomatic assignment. The Foreign Service has a ceremonial tradition called Flag Day in which new American diplomats find out their first assignment. I sat in the living room of our apartment at the desk where I had done my virtual orientation as a diplomat. And at 1:30 p.m., the virtual Flag Day ceremony started. After years of preparation and months of uncertainty, I was eager to hear what my first assignment would be. Our Foreign Service class's lead coordinator gave an address, describing us as resilient, resourceful, and ready. He praised our commitment and enthusiasm, as well as the judgment, skills, and experiences we had acquired, which would help us meet the challenges of the times as we continued our work in the Foreign Service.

A different presenter asked our class, "Are you ready for your assignment?" We unmuted our computers and shouted, "Yessss!!" My heart started beating faster and faster, *boo boom, boo boom, boo boom…*, in anticipation of the announcement of our assignments. The presenter made each position announcement as an image popped up on our computer screens showing the country and its city, the position, and the name of the officer assigned there. "Kuwait City, Kuwait, economic, Catherine B…, Dhaka, Bangladesh, consular, Monica B…" We unmuted, cheered, and clapped as people's assignments were announced. "Yay! Yay!" Halfway through, the presenter asked, "Does anyone need a bathroom break? Want to grab a donut? A cup of coffee? Should we keep going?" The answer came back, "Keep going, go, go, go!" The presenter continued, "Chanai, India, consular, Michelle M…"

After hearing some of the cheers, Ibra came out of his room and asked, "Mommy, what is this?" I told Ibra, "Come sit next to me and watch the announcements." He preferred lurking behind me and asked again, "What is this Zoom call about?" I said, "It's about telling us the countries we're going to go to for our work." He continued, "They didn't call you yet?" I answered, "Not yet." Ibra leaned over my right shoulder listening to some of the announcements for a moment, then went back to his room. About forty-eight minutes into the ceremony, the presenter called my name, "Brasilia, Brazil, political, Aminata Sy." Ibra called out, "I heard that," as I quietly clapped and smiled. A sense of relief at finally knowing the specific place where I would be working came over me, but Ibra wanted more clarification. "Mommy, where are we going?" "Brasilia, Brazil," I said. "Why are we going to Brazil?" he asked. I responded, "I'll work there, and we'll live there." And Ibra smiled; he was indeed going to be my traveling buddy at last. The ceremony ended with the presenter congratulating our class and wishing us well in our careers.

I logged out and called my husband, who was with Aissata at an orientation for twelfth graders at her new high school. "I have some breaking news!" I told him "Brasilia, Brazil, political, Aminata Sy! I got everything I asked for; Brasilia was our first choice." My husband responded, "Wow, wow, wow, congratulations!" Our conversation was brief since my husband and Aissata were touring the high school with teachers and other families.

Our class finished its six-week Foreign Service orientation on August 13, 2021, and our virtual keynote speaker for the closing ceremony was the deputy secretary of state for management and resources, Brian McKeon, who had spent a lifetime of public service in the federal government. He talked about the increasingly dangerous world and the need to protect our country; he said that persistence, creativity, teamwork, and sacrifice were expected of us. He added that all of us in some ways would become ambassadors of the United States overseas because we would interact with locals, and our actions and words would reflect on the United States as a whole. He went on to say that the Department of State was actively pushing toward diversity and inclusion and that we needed to play a role in that effort. He advised us to be open to new experiences in our careers and said, "Our future successes are yours to create."

Applying for and receiving diplomatic passports and visas were other thrilling moments.

On Friday, October 8, 2021, our three children, my husband, and I went to our appointment to begin the application process for our passports. That day, Aissata and Ibra got off school early, at 1:00 p.m. Amadou had come from Philadelphia the previous day to go to this appointment. A consular officer assisted us with the application for about forty-five minutes, processing our documents one person at a time. We took our passport photos on-site at a booth, and the same consular officer said the diplomatic passports would be ready in about four weeks. When we were done, Ibra told me, "Mommy, we came here just to take a photo?" At nine years old, Ibra didn't understand that this appointment would represent a major change in his life. From his point of view, all he did was sit for a photo, since my husband and I filled out the necessary documents for him. Amadou and Aissata signed their documents and had some sense of the importance of that moment.

That appointment was a culmination of years of work, worry, doubts, sleepless nights, and sacrifices. One of those sacrifices was choosing not to have a social life outside of my home so that I could focus on my marriage, kids, studies, and professional development. The journey was isolating because most people I knew didn't understand what I was doing. Now I was one step closer to starting a U.S. diplomatic career, which I couldn't have even dreamed about when I was growing up. How would a girl growing up in Senegal dream of becoming an American diplomat?

On the sunny afternoon of Monday, October 25, 2021, we received our U.S. diplomatic passports. During the lunch break of my Portuguese language training, my husband drove me to Washington, DC; I picked up the five passports that would take us to the first assignment in my new career. Looking at my black passport, on its first page, the U.S. Secretary of State grants me permission to travel without "hindrance" and have the necessary "protection." The line that stood out to me the most was on the third page of the passport, above my picture, which read, "The bearer is abroad on a diplomatic assignment for the United States government." I had become an official representative of America; I felt both pride in that responsibility and the weight of it.

When I got home, I paused to take in the moment with my husband, the person who had been there with me every step of this diplomatic journey. He repeated what he had said to me many times before: "You deserve it; you worked for it." I prayed that God would continue to protect me and my family and that I would carry out my diplomatic assignments for the U.S. government and the American public under his guidance and wisdom. Then I logged back into my virtual Portuguese class and carried on with my day. I knew that I had taken a major step in my diplomatic career.

I did my Portuguese training from September 2021 to February 2022, 8:00 a.m. to 3:30 p.m., along with three other colleagues, all of us heading to the U.S. Embassy in Brasilia for our assignments. Four different Portuguese instructors taught us during the six-month training period, all of them Brazilian women living in the United States and excellent teachers.

At first, I struggled quite a bit with Portuguese. I had studied Spanish in college, and now it all came back to me while learning Portuguese, which confused me instead of helping me. For example, I would translate "I am" as *soy* (Spanish) instead of *sou* (Portuguese), or "I am going" as *voy* instead of *vou*. It was hard to get used to Portuguese sounds in words like *intelligenche* (intelligent), *differenche* (different), or *futchbol* (football). It was also confusing when words changed their meaning depending on context. For example, *Ela e politica* means "She is a politician," but *politica no Brasil* means "politics in Brazil," while *Politica publica e importante* means "Public policy is important."

I listened to BBC Brasil often to get used to hearing and understanding various Portuguese accents. Brazilians have many regional accents depending on which part of the country they live in, such as in the north, south, or west. For example, some Brazilians pronounce *s* as *sss* like soup in English, and others as *sh* like *shoes*. Some pronounce a d like the d in English dog, and others like the dg in judge. Some spoke so fast that it was hard to catch a sentence amid the flow of words.

Virtual learning and the tight schedule were a challenge as well. I experienced ongoing fatigue sitting and staring at my computer screen day in and day out for hours, and I could hardly attend to the needs of my family life in the meager time available outside of my training. I spent my one-hour lunch breaks handling the logistics of our move to Brazil, such as travel arrangements and emailing back and forth with colleagues in Brasilia with regard to our airport pickup and housing arrangements. Thank goodness for my husband's extensive support and help!

As I continued to learn and practice Portuguese, I could see and hear myself improve. I did many presentations during the course of my Portuguese training. I would write the presentations, practice saying them aloud over and over, record myself, and replay the recordings to hear my pronunciation and correct my mistakes. I shared my recordings with my Portuguese instructors as well and got their feedback. I also contributed blog entries for our class, as a way of practicing the language.

I noticed that I began to understand Portuguese early in my learning process. During class, the instructors spoke in Portuguese the entire time. I paid extra attention, in an effort to understand words, phrases, or sometimes full sentences. Gradually, I began to understand much of what my instructors were saying.

For further practice, I watched and listened to BBC Brasil or CNN Brasil. After class, I usually took Ibra to play at a park near our apartment. On October 6, 2021, as Ibra played tag with other children or rode his bike, I walked around the park to stretch my legs and watched BBC Brazil on YouTube discussing Brazil's image around the world for the last decade and how it went from a promising nation to an ill-governed one. The report was nine minutes and twenty-five seconds long, and I understood about ninety-five percent of what the reporter said. I felt pride that I had already started to understand this completely new language and satisfaction that my hours of learning were paying off.

Another example of my progress in Portuguese was the presentation I did on October 15, 2021, on the film *Marighella*. The instructor projected my PowerPoint slides on the screen as I discussed them in Portuguese. The first slide introduced the film with an image of the main character, Carlos Marighella, played by actor Seu Jorge. I discussed eight key vocabulary words from the film, including *censura*, meaning censorship, and *lutar*, meaning to fight or struggle. I explained each word in detail and illustrated their meanings in context, as in the two examples below.

Censura: é uma palavra feminina que significa impedir as pessoas de falar. Por exemplo, às vezes os governos impõem censura aos jornalistas.

[*Censura*, censorship, is a feminine word that means stopping people from speaking out. For example, sometimes governments impose censorship on journalists.]

Lutar: Pode significar trabalhar duro por algo ou alguém. Por exemplo, milhões de pessoas em todo o mundo lutam para sair da pobreza.

[*Lutar*, to fight or struggle, can mean working hard for something or someone. For example, millions of people around the world fight to get out of poverty.]

I then summarized the film for the class:

O filme *Marighella* é sobre Carlos Marighella, um revolucionário brasileiro de esquerda que lutou contra a ditadura militar brasileira e denunciou seus crimes e censura. O filme se passa na década de 1960 e tem drama, suspense, violência e tensão racial. A personagem principal, Marighella, é retratada como uma lutadora pela liberdade, uma criminosa e um ser humano que tenta proteger sua família e manter uma conexão com ela. Marighella era um homem birracial, mas o personagem que o interpreta no filme é um homem negro. O filme justapõe um Estado brasileiro poderoso e brutal com Marighella e seus combatentes, retratados como vítimas e heróis.

[The film *Marighella* is about Carlos Marighella, a leftist Brazilian revolutionary who fought against the Brazilian military dictatorship and denounced its crimes and censorship. The film takes place in the 1960s and has drama, suspense, violence, and racial tension. The main character, Marighella, is portrayed as a freedom fighter, a criminal, and a human being who tries to protect his family and maintain a connection with them. Marighella was a biracial man, but the character who plays him in the film is a Black man (i.e., with no apparent admixture of European heritage). The film juxtaposes a powerful and brutal Brazilian state with Marighella and his fighters, who are portrayed as victims and heroes.]

I compared *Marighella* to the movie *Selma*.

Marighella me lembra o filme Selma, que é sobre o líder americano dos direitos civis Martin Luther King e os seus colegas que lutam pelos direitos de voto dos afro-americanos nos estados do sul dos Estados Unidos. Ambos os filmes mostram a supressão de direitos por parte do Estado e a violência contra os seus cidadãos. Ambos os filmes apresentam homens negros como personagens principais, inimigos do Estado, vítimas e heróis. Ambos os filmes têm uma produção de alta qualidade em termos de imagem e som e têm suas histórias ambientadas na década de 1960. Ambos os filmes são controversos porque denunciam publicamente e contundentemente as ações dos governos dos seus países e revelam muitos dos problemas sociais. Ambos os filmes mostram como as vidas dos personagens principais estão em constante perigo e como esses homens tentam proteger suas famílias de suas lutas. A raça também desempenha um papel fundamental nas lutas dos personagens principais por direitos e liberdade.

[*Marighella* reminds me of the movie *Selma*, which is about the American civil rights leader Martin Luther King and his colleagues fighting for the voting rights of African Americans in the South of the United States. Both films show the suppression of rights by the state and violence against its citizens. Both films feature Black men as main characters, enemies of the state, victims, and heroes. Both films are high-quality productions in terms of image and sound and portray events of the 1960s. Both films are controversial because they publicly and forcefully denounce the actions of their countries' governments and reveal many of their social problems. Both films show how the main characters' lives are in constant danger and how these men try to protect their families from their struggles. Race also plays a key role in the main characters' struggles for rights and freedom.]

I concluded by asking my colleagues six questions. Some were focused on the comprehension of the presentation. For example, who was Carlos Marighella? How was Carlos Marighella portrayed in the film? Or in Portuguese, *quem foi Carlos Marighella? Como Carlos Marighella foi retratado no filme Marighella?*

I also asked my colleagues for their opinions. Why do you think Marighella is played by a Black man in the movie when Carlos Marighella was biracial? Are you interested in watching the movie *Marighella*? If yes or no, why? Or in Portuguese, *por que você acha que no filme Marighella é interpretado por homem negro quando Carlos Marighella era birracial? Você tem interesse em assistir o filme Marighella? Se sim ou não, por quê?*

The response of my colleagues was unanimous; they all wanted to watch the film! They said that I explained the film clearly, which enticed them to want to watch it. The instructor described my presentation as detailed, deep, and analytical in comparing the films *Marighella* and *Selma*.

When I wrapped up my seventh week of Portuguese training on October 18, 2021, I discussed my areas of improvement with my second instructor. She said I was on track and making progress, paid attention to the details of the Portuguese language, focused, and asked clarification questions, all of which enhanced my learning and that of my colleagues. She advised me to go with my intuition in making sense of the language, such as asking myself to think in Portuguese and expressing myself in real-life situations as opposed to the classroom.

In late December 2021, I took my second Portuguese test and passed. Though I had made much progress by then, I still needed to improve. Portuguese has two kinds of past tenses: perfect preterite and imperfect preterite. I was still unclear on when to use each one. I was also still trying to master the agreement of nouns with their modifiers in number and gender. For example, "many places are close" would be in Portuguese "*muitos lugares estao pertos*." The gender and number of the adjectives must all agree with the noun.

My Portuguese speaking improved more than my reading. I needed to better understand texts in Portuguese and learn to summarize them in a way that better captured their main points and become more aware of the connections between paragraphs, including transition words. When reading an opinion piece in Portuguese, I needed to better articulate the argument of the text, explain its point clearly, and identify its tone.

Fast-forward to February 23, 2022. During my last Portuguese class, I shared my gratitude with my instructor and peers for my learning experience. I said that like everyone, I got frustrated here and there with the Portuguese training but that we had a great group and learning dynamic, which was encouraging to me. I said I was amazed at how much I had learned over those past few months both from the different instructors and from my peers. The following day, on February 24, 2022, from 8:40 a.m. to 10:30 a.m., I took my third and final Portuguese test and passed!

That was my first exposure to the Portuguese language, and I had made so much progress. I could understand Portuguese, express ideas, share opinions, write, and even think in the language. I could read and understand texts in Portuguese. Overall, I felt ready to use the Portuguese language to do my job in Brazil. I think what helped me the most and could help others in learning a new language was a combination of being open to learning Portuguese and liking languages in general, being willing to speak even while making many mistakes, figuring out different ways to improve, constantly practicing, asking for help when I had questions, and listening to the spoken language on an ongoing basis to become familiar with its sounds.

As my family and I were inching closer to our departure for Brazil, we still had some unresolved issues. I talked to my career development officer about a possible extension of my training time in Arlington so that my children could complete their school year, and especially so that Aissata could graduate from high school in the United States. She basically said that extending my training time in Arlington due to my children's schooling did not accord with Foreign Service policies. My only option was to negotiate with Aissata's school to figure out a solution. It took months of communication with the principal, counselor, and administrators for them to decide that Aissata could complete twelfth grade about a month and a half early to accommodate our departure for Brazil on April 6, 2022. Aissata submitted the rest of her school assignments. She didn't get credit for her advanced placement classes because those tests were administered on a date after our departure, and she didn't attend her high school graduation ceremony. She ended up receiving her high school diploma in the mail about three months after arriving in Brazil.

As for my mom, her health was relatively stable, and she could manage most of her day-to-day activities, such as getting ready for dialysis, preparing meals that met her special dietary requirements, and doing her laundry. But she couldn't manage anything administrative related to her medical care or life in America because she didn't speak English and didn't understand how the country's systems worked. For seven years, I handled her needs and wants with my husband's support. Before departing for Brazil, my husband and I moved my mom to an apartment, made sure her rent was paid each month, and made her other bills payable online, so we could pay them directly from overseas. I talked to Mom's dialysis doctor and social worker about potential caretaking support for her, which she started receiving a couple of months later. A nurse's aide later started helping her with house chores, scheduling her appointments, and accompanying her to them. I also asked two longtime family friends, who lived a few blocks away from my mom, to keep an eye on her. This was a big change for my mom; she wanted and needed me and my family close to her, but she also understood that I had to live my life. By that point, I had had many conversations with her explaining that my career would require me and my family to live overseas.

My transition to the U.S. Foreign Service took my level of patience, endurance, and faith to another level. The number of changes that were happening simultaneously in my life demanded that I be comfortable remaining in uncertainty, even completely giving up control in situations involving me and my family as we prepared for my diplomatic career. Those areas I didn't control included the country or house I and my family would live in, the schools my children attended, and the lack of clarity about what our lives would look like overseas.

In our lives, we all face adversity, even in the midst of progress. The enduring question is, how do we handle adversity, no matter what form it takes and in what context it comes? Hopefully, you won't allow adversity to deflect you from your path. You'll stare uncertainty, fear, and doubt in the face and still continue to move forward.

Chapter Ten

Our Country and Its Contradictions

AS I WRITE THESE WORDS, IT'S MONDAY, JANUARY 17, 2022, at 5:00 a.m. Outside of my bedroom in Arlington, the streets are covered with snow. The early morning hours are quiet and dark, no people walking and no cars running. I open my bedroom window on the twenty-third floor of the building, letting the whistling wind of the new day hit my face and taking in the view of snow-covered trees, roads, buildings, and the park nearby.

It's Martin Luther King Jr. Day, a holiday honoring a man who lived and died by fears and hopes for our country. He struggled against the profound and blatant racism that defined every day of his life and the lives of Black people in America through laws and policies that said he and they were less than human and didn't deserve to enjoy the fruits of our country, even though their ancestors had built America with their bare hands and blood.

MLK Day reminded me of the trip I took to the King Memorial in Washington, DC, on October 23, 2021, to pay homage to this man and to millions of others dead and alive who made my journey in the United States possible. Overlooking the Potomac River, Dr. King's statue commanded respect and was full of a calm and peaceful presence. It captured the moment in his "I Have a Dream" speech when he quoted scripture, saying that we won't be satisfied until "justice rolls down like waters, and righteousness like a mighty stream." I spent more time reading and rereading his words, which were etched on a gray stone wall. The words that Dr. King said in Alabama in 1965 stood out to me the most: "We must come to see that the end we seek is a society at peace with itself. A society that can live with its conscience."

In America, if the quality of children's education is still determined by their zip code; if people's housing, employment, and salaries are still determined by their race, gender, and national origin; if a college education is still reserved for the few and student loans still impoverish people's lives; if civil rights for the powerless are still under threat; if more individuals are incarcerated in the United States than anywhere else in the world, then our country can't live with its conscience yet. We still have work to do.

MLK Day reminded me of a tour I organized at the National Museum of African American History and Culture in Washington, DC, on June 30, 2019, and attended with other Rangel Fellows. One of the striking memories of this tour was the Emmett Till memorial. The fourteen-year-old Emmett, who lived in Chicago, was visiting family in Money, Mississippi, when he was lynched and mutilated on August 28, 1955. Some

White people had accused Emmett of whistling at a White woman; relatives of that woman kidnapped, tortured, and murdered him, and then tossed his body in a river. His murderers were acquitted of their gruesome crime by an all-White jury.

Insisting on an open-casket funeral, Emmett's mother, Mamie Till Mobley, said the world needed to witness "what they did to my boy." I saw Emmett's actual casket, which the Department of Justice had exhumed as part of their 2005 investigation of his murder. (His remains were reburied in a different casket.) I saw a photo of Emmett, a boy who could have grown up to become anything. I saw a photo of his mother, grieving for the child she would never see again, the child who was seized by people who decided they had the right to kill him because he was Black and therefore his life had no value. Mobley was right; we needed to witness the crimes committed in our country.

MLK Day reminded me too of a private tour I took of the Supreme Court of the United States on July 1, 2019. Standing at the lectern, facing the justices' seats, before which lawyers argue their cases, I imagined civil rights lawyer Thurgood Marshall arguing in the case of *Brown v. Board of Education of Topeka, Kansas* in 1954, a landmark ruling that declared segregated public schools unconstitutional. I imagined the many other legal battles fought in that space that have shaped our country—for civil rights, women's rights, immigrants' rights, and reform of the criminal justice system.

MLK Day reminded me of how for days during the summer of 2020, after a police officer choked George Floyd, a Black American, to death, I could barely breathe, think, rest, sleep, or process the sorrow and the weight of racism, blatant and hidden in plain sight, that Black people in America live through in neglected neighborhoods throughout the country, as in Philadelphia. The violence inflicted upon George Floyd and his murder could happen to any Black person anywhere in the country. I worried about the lives of my children every day. Would my eighteen-year-old son be safe walking to a friend's house a few blocks away from our home? Would my sixteen-year-old daughter be safe walking to a bus stop two blocks away to catch a bus for school? Would my eight-year-old son be safe playing at a playground near our home? Life's routine activities became a constant source of worry because children were hurt and killed all the time in our neighborhood and elsewhere. Living became an act of courage; hypervigilance became the norm; staying off the streets became a way of life.

MLK Day reminded me of the poem I wrote and recited for about 100 colleagues on August 12, 2021, during our six-week orientation as we started our diplomatic careers.

Our America

"Being American is more than a pride we inherit, it's the past we step into and how we repair it."—Amanda Gorman

Dear colleagues, what America have we stepped into?
We've stepped into an America that has treated
*   Black people as less than human,*
has treated women as second-class citizens,
has treated immigrants as others.
Dear colleagues, what America have we stepped into?
We've stepped into an America that has
*   elected a Black president twice,*

has a woman vice president,
has welcomed immigrants from around the world.
Dear colleagues, we've stepped into an
   American past, present, future
that's dark and bright,
pessimistic and optimistic,
closed and open,
divided and united,
hurt and healed.
We represent all of that America through our
   stories, journeys, and identities.
Dear colleagues, how will we show up for America?
How will we carry the torch of our history
   forward as we shape history?
The answer is ours.

I am moved by the shared human experience—mine and that of others—knowing that our stories are intertwined, our achievements, challenges, pains, and injustices all interconnected. Our journeys, backgrounds, skin colors, origins, religions, and financial statuses may differ, but our humanity is the same. Our aspirations for our lives and that of our children are similar. Our desires to live dignified and fulfilling lives are similar. We all have similar capacities for evil and good. Some questions we must answer about our lives are: How am I going to show up? How do I want to live my days, weeks, months, and years on this earth? What do I value, and how do I manifest that daily in my life?

There were times in my life when I questioned how I could feel so much sorrow for the pains of people I had never met and will never meet. Over the years, I've changed that question to, how *can't* we feel sorrow for the pains of people we never met and will never meet? Systems, laws, and policies are created by people; therefore, individuals are responsible for their consequences. Even when we have nothing to do with creating those systems, laws, and policies, we can feel empathy for those suffering from them and potentially contribute to changing them.

Today in America, millions of people live in poverty. Nearly two million people are jailed in our criminal justice system, many of whom never had a chance to choose a different path or were wrongfully convicted. Black men and women are constantly killed by police. Many students of color and immigrants are set up to fail in our education system. Homeless people are sleeping and begging on our streets. Migrants are rushing to our borders to escape horrors in their countries and in the hope of a better future, only to encounter a cold welcome or even death in our care. Even immigrants who entered the country legally are often mistreated and constantly reminded that they don't belong. Many families are living in neighborhoods so steeped in crime that children can't have a childhood and reaching their eighteenth birthdays becomes an achievement. Many children are either depending on their schools for meals or go hungry. Many parents are working full-time, sometimes even two jobs, but still falling short of money to pay their bills and take care of their families.

It's our collective responsibility, the powerful and powerless, to connect to the pains of people we never met and will never meet and to demand change for our sake, for their sake, for the sake of future generations, for the sake of our country's survival. As an American diplomat, I'm going to represent our country and its many contradictions—that in America an immigrant can go from nothing to becoming a face the United States presents to the world, even as she herself embodies the many oppressions of our system, past and present. These contradictions say something about the greatness of our country and its weakness. The challenge is to remember that these realities coexist and that we must embrace both the beauty and the ugliness of our country while working to repair the ugliness and enhance the beauty, so that one day, America can live with its conscience.

Chapter Eleven

How to Achieve Against All Odds

IT'S APRIL 6, 2022. ONCE AGAIN I STAND AT AN AIRPORT, waiting to embark on a new journey. Only this time the situation is different. I'm about to start a dream career that I have worked toward for years. With my husband and children, I'm departing for Brazil from Ronald Reagan Washington National Airport. We're flying first to Miami, then to São Paulo, and finally to Brasilia, where I'll serve as a U.S. diplomat for the next two years.

I never thought that one day I would travel to Brazil or temporarily live there. I never thought that I would learn to speak Portuguese. Yet I've already grasped the fundamentals of the language, and I'm prepared to speak it in-country. I'm not nervous or scared; instead, I look forward to all the adventures ahead of us. My life has trained me for this moment. Just like a plane, I'm ready to fly to my next destination in life. For me, that's just a start; I know that I'll continue to dream, learn, and grow.

It takes courage to become—the courage to start, continue, and persist, no matter what.

In the words of the Ashanti people of Ghana, "Do not follow the path. Go where there is no path to begin the trail." That is, know that you can create your own path, one that reflects what you want for your life. I define courage as doing something that terrifies you and persisting while having no guarantee that you'll get the outcome you hope for, going for it against the odds and at the risk of being misunderstood and lonely in that effort.

There was no way I could have dreamed of becoming a U.S. diplomat. I never even thought that one day I would immigrate to the United States until I married my husband, who already lived there. I never thought of a career in diplomacy until I was a student at community college. Before then, I didn't have the connections, guidance, resources, knowledge, or an environment that would encourage me to consider it. People will tell you that you can't achieve your dreams; your life circumstances will tell you that you can't achieve your dreams; your own fears and doubts will tell you that you can't achieve your dreams. But I ask you to have the courage to push through adversities and work on your dreams one day at a time. As you work on your dreams, you'll attract the right people into your life to support your efforts. Commit yourself to learning and improving daily and building the discipline and focus to do what you need to do when you need to do it. Develop the resilience to stick with your journey, not just on the sunny days, but on the rainy, or even stormy, ones.

It takes courage to change your life. I wanted to break the cycle of poverty in my life and that of my family. I also wanted to pursue a career that no one in my family had ever had and to travel the world to connect with new people and cultures and expand my perspective. Each one of these goals has taken ongoing courage for me to achieve. If you want to change your life, you'll have to make room for the new circumstances that you desire. This change doesn't mean that you'll forget who you are or won't appreciate your background anymore; it simply means that you want something more and different for your life.

It takes courage to become someone new. I went through a long period of isolation and loneliness because I returned to school as a high school dropout and went all the way to a master's degree, and no married woman with children in my African immigrant community in Philadelphia had done that before. While a college student, I explored careers as a journalist and nonprofit leader. And people close and distant misunderstood me and even distanced themselves from me because I embarked on a path they never thought possible for me or for themselves. Still, set big goals and dreams, and dare to stand out by pursuing and realizing them, because we each have something specific to us that we need to accomplish and contribute.

It takes courage to face fear and grow. I was petrified by the thought of failing when I started pursuing an associate's degree at community college. I was an English learner with a weak academic background, didn't know how to be a college student, had no money to pay for my education, and was a married mother of three with many responsibilities. But I decided to go for it anyway, though I doubted that I would stick around for even a week of school, let alone earn a degree. You won't know what can happen in your life unless you're willing to try.

The beauty is that when we try to pursue goals and dreams that scare us, we learn just how capable we are as human beings and that we can overcome limitations and become someone we never could have imagined.

It takes courage to be different. For me, being different has meant many things: being an immigrant; having an accent and an "unusual" name; being multilingual; committing to lifelong learning; and working on issues that I'm passionate about, such as those related to education and immigrants, pursuing dreams and goals that seem impossible, being the first in my family to do most of the things that I've done. Many aspects of ourselves and our life experiences make us different, and that difference is our offering to the world. So embrace your authentic self, with all its unusualness.

It takes courage to make risky decisions. After giving birth to my first child, doctors told me that I would be risking my life if I got pregnant again. But I chose to continue to have children anyway, because that's what I wanted for my life, even at the risk of losing it. Doctors are human beings like me, not God, who alone can decide my destiny. Being the mother of three children has been the biggest blessing of my life. There will be times when people will discourage you from pursuing something that gives meaning to your life. In those situations, do what you believe is right for you.

It takes courage to take responsibility for your life. I got to a point where I had to decide if I wanted to carry for the rest of my life the pain of the separation from my parents at ten years old and the experiences of growing up in poverty and constant trauma. Around the age of twenty-seven, I decided to forgive those who had hurt me in my childhood and began my healing process. From then on, a heavy weight began to lift off of me. When you fully take responsibility for your life, you stop making excuses for yourself and blaming other people who wronged you. Instead, you forgive those who hurt you and take your healing into your own hands. You don't wait for motivation and inspiration to act. Instead, you build the necessary discipline to execute your plans. When things fail, it's on you, and when things work out, it's also on you.

I didn't speak English until I immigrated to America and started learning it through my jobs and now have written this book to share my story with you. Dark times will come in our lives; they may even be prolonged. But that doesn't mean that we can never overcome them and that our circumstances will never improve. At some point, everything comes to an end in our lives. Our lives themselves will end. You're destined to achieve extraordinary things. What actions do you want to take in your life today that could change your tomorrow? What contributions do you want to make? Who do you want to become in your life, and why?

I want to leave you with this: what is meant for you in your life is yours, which means no one and nothing can get in its way, not adversity and not difficult people. Your path is yours to walk, so give life your best and author your story one page at a time, one chapter at a time, for you, your family, and generations to come. There's nothing in my background that could have predicted my journey from dropping out of high school to earning a master's degree to serving as an American diplomat. I hope that my story can inspire you to push through major adversities, dare to transform your life, and believe that life is full of possibilities. I wish you the courage to live out your destiny.

Acknowledgments

THIS IS A MESSAGE OF GRATITUDE TO THE PEOPLE WHO shared this journey with me, those who helped make it happen, and the higher power that has guided my life.

TO GOD

You've guided me throughout my darkest times. You've protected me through the good and the bad. You've connected me with people of wonderful character. You've blessed me continually, and you've always been there with me and for me. Thank you for everything.

TO MY PARENTS

Mom and Dad, when I separated from you at the age of ten, I had no clue that, from then on, I would have to figure out answers for my life on my own. I went through years of grief, loneliness, confusion, and pain because you gave me away to grow up in a faraway place where I knew no one and nothing was familiar. I forgive you for all the years of pain. I forgive you for giving up on your responsibilities as my parents. I forgive you for all the traumas that I went through in your absence. Because of you, I decided that I wanted to be a parent who is present in my children's lives. Separating from you has not been the hardest experience of my life; raising my children has been the hardest, and in many ways, you prepared me for that. Thank you for bringing me into this world. Dad, may your soul continue to rest in peace. Mom, may God allow you to live long enough to experience every blessing meant for you.

TO YAYE

Yaye, you raised me from nothing and poured everything you could into me. It's been many years since you passed away, but every day, I still feel your presence with me. Thank you for all of the life lessons you taught me: perseverance, patience, generosity, resilience, adaptability, and service to others. More than anything, I learned from you that the meaning of life lies in the people we invest in. And often that investment doesn't require spending any money; it requires heart, willingness, and commitment. Thank you so much; may you continue to rest in peace.

TO MY HUSBAND

I'm blessed to share my life with you. Your generosity, your sense of responsibility as a husband and father, and your beautiful heart as a human being make you an outstanding person. We've dealt with so many ups and downs, yet together we've managed to talk through and overcome many challenges. May we continue to have long conversations; may we continue to share laughter; may we continue to take good care of our children; may we continue to support one another and other people along the way. Thank you so much for giving me the space and peace of mind to grow and for being a blessing to my life and those of our children.

TO MY CHILDREN

It's because of you that I want better living conditions for our family and a better world. You fill me with joy and hope; you push me to pursue goals and dreams that scare me. You teach me about the beauty of life and help me distinguish between what's important and what's not. You challenge me to improve; you remind me of how far we've come as a family and how far we still need to go. You stretch my level of patience; you show me the miracles of God. I'm blessed to be your mother. Thank you for all the shining lights that you've brought into my life. May you remain kind and decent human beings. May you receive all the blessings meant for you. May God continue to protect and guide you.

TO MY SUPPORTERS

You've helped pull me through some of the most challenging times of my life. Some of you supported me in my childhood and during my teenage years as I navigated many hardships. Some of you helped me academically through tutoring, advising, providing me guidance about how to participate in extracurricular activities, answering my many questions, or introducing me to resources that contributed to my growth. Some of you supported me in my professional endeavors, including my leadership of ACLP, my work as a journalist, and my career in diplomacy. Some of you helped me bring this book to existence. You know who you are; I thank you all for your investments and for believing in me. I pray that I make you proud.

About the Author

AMINATA SY is a leader who served as a U.S. diplomat in Brazil and a congressional fellow working on education policy in the U.S. Senate. In *Destined: A Story of Resilience and Beating the Odds*, Aminata shares her journey, providing an intimate look at life as a mother juggling school and work in pursuit of a rewarding career and a better life for her family. Narrated with humility and candor, *Destined* is an inspirational memoir reminding us that each challenge makes us stronger, each goal makes us wiser, and no dream is too far out of reach.

Aminata has inspired thousands throughout her journey, accumulating an overall seventeen years of experience in the fields of international affairs, education, entrepreneurship, and journalism. When she arrived in the United States in 2001, she was a high school dropout who did not speak English but has since gone on to earn a master's degree and is among the few Senegalese Americans to serve as a U.S. diplomat and the first married woman in her African immigrant community in West Philadelphia to attend college, pursue journalism, or enter the field of diplomacy. She has been described as an inspiration, trailblazer, and changemaker.

Aminata trained in American diplomacy through the U.S. Department of State Rangel Graduate Fellowship Program. She reported and wrote for different publications in Philadelphia, Pennsylvania, focusing on the stories of Black Americans and African immigrants. In 2017, she founded the African Community Learning Program, a nonprofit organization, and led it for four years. There she created a culturally responsive curriculum, taught English to African diaspora students and supported them as they integrated into American society, wrote policy documents for Philadelphia public officials, and led at least 165 volunteers. She is the founder and CEO of Aminata Sy Enterprises, LLC, where, through her story, she teaches, writes, and speaks about achieving greatness against all odds. She speaks English, French, Portuguese, Pulaar, Wolof, and some Spanish.

Aminata's story and her perspectives on education have been featured in numerous publications, including the *Philadelphia Inquirer* and *Chalkbeat*. She has received many awards and honors for leadership, academic excellence, and contributions to society, including a Philadelphia Mayoral Citation. She was named among Philadelphia's Most Influential by the *Philadelphia Tribune* and as a Woman of Influence by *FunTimes* magazine.

She holds a master's degree in public policy from American University; a bachelor's degree in international relations, cum laude with distinction, from the University of Pennsylvania; and an associate's degree in international studies, with highest honors, from Community College of Philadelphia.

www.ingramcontent.com/pod-product-compliance
Lightning Source LLC
Chambersburg PA
CBHW030519080526
44586CB00011B/255